MW01118163

ISBN 987-1-59872-925-2
Instantpublisher.com, Collierville,TN

Notes from

Our Sylvilla

"Our House at the Edge of the Woods"

6604 Rolling Fork Dr.

1964 - 1984

Charlotte Marie Boone Perry (1926-2005)

Old Log House

James S. Tippet

Forever and ever

I wish I could

Live in a house

At the edge of a wood.

"Sylvilla" - Latin for house at the edge of the wood.
Grandpa King gave this name to the house he and
Martha Sarah Sills built after the Civil War on property
left to her by her father, Dr. Gray Sills of "Belford."

.

I was born there at the edge of the wood in "Sylvilla II."

Our Sylvilla

6604 Rolling Fork Drive

I was a busy mother with four children, but as the two older girls, Elizabeth and Martha Sills, became more independent, there seemed to be more time to run for a pencil and scrap of paper to record a few of the children's sayings and memorable activities. Here are some, which I recorded from time to time so that I would not forget. Recently, I discovered many of them tucked away in a notebook, and I thought it might amuse my offspring as grownups to review some of the things with which they amused me when they were children. There is no chronological order - just recorded at random discovery. I have also included things I wrote from time to time about our surroundings and my feelings of appreciation at the moment.

* * *

In the spring of 1964, George called me from Nashville, Tennessee, to say that he was on the board of directors of Diamond Hill Plywood Company of Darlington, S.C., and that they had a branch in Greensboro where Elizabeth, Martha Sills, James and I lived. "Would it be all right if I come to see you on my next trip over there?" To me it sounded interesting to see my old friend again. The children were very excited about it.

At school Martha Sills, aged 7, told her teacher, "We're going to have company this weekend!"

Teacher said, "You are? Who?"

Martha: "His name is George G. Perry, Jr. He's from Nashville, Tennessee; he's an old friend of my mother; she hasn't seen him in 7 years, and he's coming this weekend to look us over!" You see, she wanted a father more than anything in the world!

When I told her that her own father had died, she responded immediately while sitting in my lap in our Dallas kitchen: "But now, Mommy, we won't have a husband! When can we get another one? Who's going to cook the steaks?"

When we came to Greensboro to live, Martha immediately fell in love with her Uncle "Rip" Vann Burgess. Her next crush was Lloyd Bridges on TV. Then came the Dallas Cowboys! And Roger Staubach . . .

The weekend that George came for a visit, he ate Saturday morning breakfast with the children and me. They entertained him in the living room while I fixed breakfast. I overheard James, aged 3, call George "Daddy."

It seems that Elizabeth had told him to do that. They were all three working on getting George for their new father. He loved all of it!

At the Chinese restaurant at lunch on Sunday, the girls each read her fortune cookie's prediction; then I read mine, and George saved his for last. We all, especially the girls and I, waited with "bated breath" to hear George read his fortune. It said, "Wait for a better opportunity." How he laughed! But he did not wait very long.

In August we were married at St. Andrews Episcopal Church. Mr. Herman, the rector who had watched over the children and me for three years, "warned" George that he must be good and faithful, sincere and loving to this precious little family. He was not about to let "just anybody" have us!

Elizabeth was, perhaps, the most reluctant to leave Greensboro and go to live in Nashville, where she had been born nine years before. George said, "Come on and go to live in Nashville, and I'll teach you to eat grits." She cried! George was not exactly a girl-charmer, but he was an enthusiastic father who took great pride in the children and provided a good home for us all for almost 30 years thereafter.

We left Pearly Mae and Silas ("Pearlie Maid and Silence, as little cousin Vann called them), Aunt Martha, Uncle "Rip," Jenny, Vann and a host of friends in Greensboro and headed for our new Nashville home in late August.

On the west side of Knoxville, James, age 3, who was tired of riding, told George he needed to go to the bathroom. George gave a right hand signal in the new blue Dodge in which the two of them were riding, and the girls and I in our little Chevy station wagon pulled off the interstate behind them. Soon we were westward bound again, and soon George signaled <u>again</u> that they were making an exit. The same excuse from the 3-year-old boy! He had already learned to manipulate his new father, who was much amused.

Around 4 p.m. we arrived at 6604 Rolling Fork Drive, the home that was to be ours for more than thirty years. It was a lovely haven on a hillside for all of us, pretty and safe on a dead end street with a cul de sac surrounded by steep hills and large trees.

George, a Colonel in the U.S.A.R., had Army Reserve meetings every Monday night, and he taught James to march and present arms. To have an army colonel dressed in uniform to call the cadence was music to the little boy's ears. The two of them put on a show for us every Monday night at dinner.

When George went to choir practice on the first Wednesday evening, the children ran up and down the hillside in the August moonlight amidst myriads of fireflies. It was wonderful fun to watch them in their late August frolics until the headlights of the new father's automobile turned into the driveway. We all felt like a real family again.

School started soon and the girls waited for the school bus at the corner of Rolling Fork Court and Rolling Fork Drive. When I picked them up in the station wagon in the afternoon, they wanted me to take them to the top of the hill on Rolling Fork. The Watson boys had placed a Highway 70S sign at the bottom of the hill, so I gunned the motor and climbed the high hill to find only a row of mailboxes waiting instead of a highway.

There were four families living at the summit: the Williamsons, the Crists, the Watsons and the Engles.

When it rained one morning in early September, James and I took the girls to the school bus stop in the station wagon to wait. A little car went up Rolling Fork Court, hastily returned, turned left on Rolling

Fork Drive, came quickly back, turned right and scooted up Rolling Fork Court again.

The bus came and picked up the girls; the little car came back to the corner, stopped, and the man rolled down his window. So did I. He asked rather frantically, "Lady, can you tell me how to get out of here?"

I showed him to turn right and follow the school bus, and I thoroughly appreciated how isolated we were in that lovely wooded setting. It felt good to us to be in our new home.

One late summer evening, George and I sat on the back porch after dinner, facing the hill to the northeast and looking at the rising full moon in the eastern sky. James was riding his tricycle back and forth looking at the moon. He said, "I see the man in the moon! He's wiggling his nose!" George already loved the children's observations on life!

A few weeks later, after his Sunday afternoon nap, James entered the den sleepily wiping his eyes and pointed to the black and white TV on which a pro football game was going. "Just look at those 'coons'!" he said. I knew that George had already shared some of his prejudiced Alabama lingo with my son, and I let him know in no uncertain terms that my children were

Day Lilies Viewed from Back Porch

<u>not</u> to be subjected to that sort of prejudicial lingo again!

We were soon feeling much at home on Rolling Fork Drive, and I decided while Martha and Elizabeth were in school to take three-year-old James into downtown Nashville (9 miles) to an established photographer to have his picture made. It turned out that the elderly photographer was very unsmiling and distant in personality. He matter-of-factly set James in position. Then he reached into a mound of toys, picked one up, shook it in front of James and said, "Smile."

James sat there observing the goings on and looked as solemn as a judge. The photographer picked up another toy, waved it in the air at the unsmiling boy and said, "Smile," all the while looking very unsmiling himself. He then repeated these antics another time or so and received the same results from James. Now the man showed his disdain - so - James lifted his arm, pointed to a toy and said, "Why don't you try <u>that</u> one?"

He did, and James smiled! Just right!

* * *

Life soon became a flurry of going to school, going to music lessons, baseball, basketball and football practices and games, tennis lessons, orchestra practices, PTA meetings, Sunday school, birthday parties and the myriad things that involve bringing up four children.

When George found out that he was going to be a father (48 years old) he said it did not matter whether we had a boy or a girl. On the beautiful morning of June 10, 1965, we took James to stay with his friend, Tommy and headed to the old St. Thomas Hospital to have our baby. Elizabeth and Martha Sills had gone to North Carolina to visit Aunt Martha.

When George left me at the elevator with a nurse to go upstairs to have the baby, he said with a lovely smile and a cheery voice, "Go get that boy!"

And so, we added Graham to our family.

Four children there were about a year after George and I were married. We were all blessed with the arrival of George Graham Perry, III. We put him in a long antique walnut cradle from Kentucky, and he became a wonderful part of the family immediately. Nobody was quiet just for him. He was picked up from a deep sleep to go with us to music lessons, always a part of the family goings on.

One afternoon I picked up the sleeping baby, put him on the front seat of the station wagon, loaded the other children and the cello, and took off for Blair

Academy for Elizabeth's cello lesson with Mr. Harvey Wolfe. James, aged about five by this time, was in the back seat jumping wildly up and down as I turned into Davidson Road from Jocelyn Hollow. He paid no attention to my demands that he calm down and sit still. I had heard that dashing water into a child's face would put a stop to such antics. As I was getting into heavy 4:30 p.m. traffic I decided to teach James a lesson. I simply threw the iced tea I was drinking over my shoulder into his face and - - to my horror a piece of ice went right into his open mouth! Fortunately, it came right back out, but it taught me a lesson! No hasty, unconsidered moves like that again with my children!

The children and I had faithfully attended the Episcopal church before we came to live in Nashville. George was a dyed-in-the-wool Presbyterian and had sung in the Westminster choir for twenty-five years, so the children were excited to go to church with their new father.

One day we were riding around to see our new city. Martha Sills was standing behind George (no seatbelt requirements in those days), and as we rode along, she was showing off her reading skills. We came to a stop, and Martha proudly read, "Stop for Presbyterians."

George proudly took Elizabeth, Martha Sills and James to Sunday school at Westminster Presbyterian Church where he had sung in the choir for 25 years. I stayed at home to relax from my weekly chores and renew my spirits with music and a good, soaking bath. After hearing The Westminster Choir sing their anthem via radio, I played my two favorite pieces of music, Brahms' "Academic Festival Overture" and <u>Beethoven's 7th Symphony</u>. This was my Sunday ritual.

* * *

I hope the following tidbits and little vignettes will give lots of pleasure to the family members who read them. You were a much-loved, active, intelligent and amusing family, and I enjoyed being your mother, despite the long, busy hours, night and day, spent trying to answer your needs. George was the most supportive father in the world, and he loved this role, which came to be his at age 48 years. No father was ever more entertained by and pleased with his children.

* * *

Elizabeth was born "ahead of the game." At six months I was astonished when she was lying on a blanket on the floor while I was talking to a visitor. When I looked, she was sitting up, by herself.

At nine months and two weeks she was walking.

At 18 months she could put on her shoes <u>and</u> buckle them. (Mary Janes)

At two and a half years she begged us to play Greig, "The Hall of the Mountain King."

When I had Elizabeth, my first child, I saw an opportunity to let her hear the best, the most correct grammar, to hear the best music, and to know the best of everything, as I saw it. We started with the use of the two verbs "to lie" and "to lay," so often misused by so many people.

After we moved from New York to Dallas, Elizabeth, aged four, was able to have friends in the neighborhood and to cross the dead-end street to visit them.

One day my four-year old came bursting through the front door and asked loudly, "Mother, is it 'lie' or 'lay'?" I said, "Calm down, honey; I would have to know <u>how</u> it was being used, but I suspect (after having heard Texans talking for the last few weeks) you mean 'lie.'"

"I <u>knew</u> it! I knew it! Tommy's record is <u>wrong</u>! It says, "The little Lord Jesus <u>lay</u> down his sweet head'!"

Her father, sitting nearby to hear this exchange

said to me, "It serves you right!" And we laughed at the whole situation!

* * *

When Elizabeth went to kindergarten at St. John's Episcopal School in Dallas, she began to learn Spanish. One afternoon she came home from school and asked me if I knew several different words in Spanish. When I said I didn't, she said, "It looks to me like you're going to have to study Spanish again!"

Back in Greensboro when she began playing cello at school in the fourth grade, I suspected that Elizabeth might have the gift of 'perfect pitch." One of my students at Grimsley High School where I worked as guidance counselor suggested that I ring the door bell and ask Elizabeth to tell me which notes they were. I could hardly wait to get home and try that!

At supper-time while the children were at the table. I opened the front door and rang the bell. I asked, "Elizabeth, do you know what those two notes are?"

She tossed off my question with, "I don't know - E and C, I think."

I rushed to the piano sitting there in the living room between us and played E and C. Sure enough! She had identified them correctly.

Always she was a very good student in school. In Greensboro in the third grade she went into an accelerated class for gifted students. That year she also began to play the cello and was chosen to be "concert mistress" for the elementary orchestra.

Elizabeth joined the Girl Scouts, and one day as we were returning from heir meeting, two friends were singing a Girl Scout song. Elizabeth said, "You're not singing in the <u>right</u> key!"

"Well, you put it in the right pitch," I said.

Immediately she changed the key, and all three happily sang as we rode down Jocelyn Hollow to Rolling Fork and home.

She went on to college at Virginia Intermont in Bristol, Virginia, because she had finished all of her high school requirements except senior English. So, she was accepted into college without a high school diploma.

* * *

When Martha Sills was three, we left her and Elizabeth with Mother and Daddy for a week while Al and I went to New York. Mother tried very hard to get Martha Sills to let her give her a bath every day. Martha insisted that she would bathe herself. So, finally, Mother gave up and let her do her own bathing the whole week - until -

The night before we were to come back Mother decided that Daddy should come to the bathroom with her to give Martha a good bath. Martha Sills stood firmly up on her own two feet while Mother knelt down to do the bathing for her. No luck! She insisted on doing her own.

From her kneeling position Mother said in exasperation, "Children, God bless them; God love them; God keep them" - - And from Martha Sills a finishing touch, "And God Damn them." She has always been perceptive!

Daddy said he practically had to pick Mother up off the floor!

* * *

When James was first learning to say words and identify objects, I loved to hold him on my lap while turning pages in the Little Folks' Golden Dictionary and pointing to objects for him to say, "ball", "tree", "boy", "bird," etc. One day I saw the picture of a globe and pointed to it. James said, without hesitation, "As the World Turns." You see, he and Pearly Mae, the maid who kept him while I was at school every day,

<u>always</u> watched "As the World Turns," a long-running TV soap opera.

* * *

I was looking at a TV program today which explored "a child's fears." "Most all children have fears which they very often fail to express. Find out what your child is afraid of. Ask in such a way that you don't discourage their telling you the truth."

I could not wait to find out what my children were afraid of. Tonight when I went to each child's room to say prayers with them before going to bed, I was as subtle as I knew how to be.

In James's room, I kissed him good night and said, "Mother thinks that sometimes children might be afraid of something and have not told anyone about it. Are you afraid of anything you can think of, James?"

"Yes, Mother, I'm afraid of <u>two</u> things." My five year old son was about to tell me something very important!

"Can you tell Mother what they are?"

"Yes, I'm afraid of <u>acne</u> and <u>amblyopia</u>."

I said, as calmly as I knew how in spite of my inclination to show how amused I was, "Well, James, I think it will be a long time before you have to be concerned about acne, and maybe never. But Mother doesn't know what amblyopia is. Could you tell me?"

"Well, when children have an eye or eyes that move about, they have amblyopia. I saw it on television."

From James's room and my best assurances, I went in to say goodnight to Martha Sills. Trying to seem as if I had just thought of it, I said as I started out of the room, "Martha, honey, Mother wonders if you are ever afraid of anything in particular."

"Not really," she said. But as I turned to go out she added, "Is there any such thing as the 'abominable snowman'?"

Just think; if I hadn't asked, I would never have known about James's and Martha's fears!

* * *

Christmas Nursery School Program, December 1969 - Westminster School - - Graham sang "Santa Claus is coming to 'Nursery school' every time others sang 'town'.

He carried a star swinging from a stick, suspended on a string. When they began to sing beside the manger, Graham turned the stick around, faced the group and conducted them with his improvised baton! (Momentarily, that is, until the teacher turned him back around.)

On the way home he said, "Daddy, do you know what? I watched Santa Claus's mouth and do you know what? It was drawn up like a bow(l)! And he had a little round belly like a bowl full of jelly, too!"

* * *

When asked for underclothes, Graham wanted "Fruit of Balloon".

He called mayonnaise "Bandaidse".

* * *

George was so happy to get invited to take his four-year-old son, Graham, along with his nursery school class at Westminster for a visit to see the farm animals at the Rudy's farm.

At the farm when the proud peacock spread himself into a grand strut, Graham exclaimed, "he's psychedelic!"

George came home amazed at his son and asked me, "What in the hell is 'psychedelic'?" He was on a new learning spiral with his growing-up son!

* * *

Graham crawled into bed with Martha at 5:30 Christmas morning. She said, "Close your eyes and go to sleep. It's too early to get up." He said, "I've got my eyes closed but I don't have any visions of sugar plums dancing in my head."

* * *

You can imagine how I felt when James came home

from day camp at five years old and said, "Mom, yesterday Chris (the counselor) was 16 years old and he got his driver's license. He took us to ride, and when he got on the interstate, he said, "Boys, we're on the freeway. Put your arms out of the window and we're gonna fly!" Oh, me!

He also was awarded first place as "Camper of the Week." "Why did you get that honor, James?" I asked.

"Because I dug the latrines, Mother!"

* * *

Fog was occasionally apt to cover us in the hills and valleys of Rolling Fork Drive. One particularly foggy morning not too long after we had come to live there, James went out on the front stoop in the shroud of fog. He rubbed his eyes vigorously, then turned to me in the doorway and said, "It's a bad picture out today."

We were in those days quite accustomed to having to adjust our "foggy" black and white 1950's TV set.

* * *

5 years old - James

When I picked James up after kindergarten at Hillwood Presbyterian Church one noon, he began immediately to tell me his story of woe. Sadly he said, "The teacher made me sit on a <u>log</u> at playtime today."

"Well, I'm sure she had a good reason." I answered with parental certainty. "I'm glad she did."

"Would you want your little boy to sit on a log with a nail in it?" So plaintively said, I really did feel his hurt! Little boys can be so easily misunderstood and offended!

* * *

The three-year-old James and I were enjoying a morning's trip to the Tennessee State Fair while the girls were at school in September. We came to a display of baby chickens, yellow, fluffy little creatures all huddled together and making lots of peeping sounds. The old lady who owned them sat in a chair watching closely as the excited little 3-year-old boy pointed to them and said, "Hamsters!"

The lady was some kind of startled. "How did he know they were Hampshires?"

I just smiled sweetly like any proud mother, and we walked on!

* * *

When James played his first football game at age six in Shelby Park one cold, dew-filled morning, he made a score.

That night when I went in to kiss him goodnight and tuck him in bed, he said from his pillow, "You know, Mother, I <u>can still feel</u> what it was like when I kept on <u>pushing hard</u> to get the ball over that goal line!"

* * *

Hopes: I hope to be able to help people in the future as well as now in some

      way.

Worries: I have no worries for I believe that for bad there is good as long as

      you try to make it that way.

Joys: My real joy is being <u>independent</u> to do what I want.

Graham Perry

Sept 3, 1980

My own observations on our family life and surroundings

* * *

August 16, 1972

Life in these United States Editor

Reader's Digest

Pleasantville, New York

   Being a native of a neighboring state, I found myself at amusing odds with my Tennessee born and bred washing machine repairman. He was visibly shaken at my action when, in the process of checking out the faulty mechanism recently, he asked me to get him the 'cheer."

I hastened to get the detergent he had requested and said, as I handed him the box, "I don't have any Cheer, but I hope you can use this Cold Power!"

Momentarily speechless, he stared at me as if I had lost my mind. Finally he stammered, "La...lady, I said I want the 'cheer'. I want to <u>stand</u> on it so I can reach the top of this dryer." To which I could only reply sheepishly, "Oh! A chair!"

Charlotte Perry
6604 Rolling Fork Drive
Nashville, Tennessee 37205

* * *

Feb. 4, 1965

Dear Mrs. Eden,

Thank you for showing us around. My mother goes to Krogers just abought every day. I liked every compartment. When we went to the meat compartment I didn't like it there so much because I had just fenish lunch. Thank you again.

Love,

Martha Jennings

Mrs. Frank's 2 Grade

Westmede School

* * *

1970

Aged 5 years old

Graham: I'll bet when Nixon dies, they'll bury him in front of the White House.

Mother: What makes you think so?

Graham: Cause when Andrew Jackson died, they buried him in front of <u>his</u> house!

* * *

October 13, 1970

James: "I sometimes think my front teeth need a 'winter coat' when I drink <u>cold</u> things!"

To George:

James, after trying out for the Vendredi program: "Right now I am number 1. I'm the only one who has tried out!"

* * *

James - aged nine, after having played Mozart in the Vendredi concert at Alexander Heard's (Chancellor of Vanderbilt University) large, columned house:

"What does a <u>Chancellor</u> do for a living?"

* * *

James: (on subject of Graham) "You got gypped when you had him. I'd go and get my money back."

* * *

Martha: (upon hearing that Catholics once had to bury limbs they lost so that they could be buried <u>beside</u> them) "At the same time?!"

* * *

Martha: (upon hearing that the superintendent of schools might not live) "If he does die, will they do away with the Metro schools?"

* * *

"A <u>full</u> professor coming out from breakfast!" (Rubbing his "poked out" tummy) Graham

* * *

About 4 years old -
Margaret reminded me of James's answer when George told him if he didn't eat right, his teeth would fall out (lose them). "Oh, I won't lose them; I'll keep my mouth shut!"

* * *

James (age 9 years, approximately) to Alys Venable, who taught him and helped him to skin and preserve a copperhead: (when he finished) - "Mrs. Venable, you have tested my "metal."

It was our good fortune to have the most wonderful neighbors, Alys and Jack Venable, next door. She was a teacher of English at the University School, and he was a molecular biologist at Vanderbilt. They were a built-in source of information for all of us.

One Sunday morning around eight o'clock the phone rang to awaken us. It was Alys, who said, "Come over here as soon as you can, all of you! There is a duel going on here on the patio between a copperhead and a king snake."

We were "up and over there" as soon as we could dress. The fight went on hour after hour until about 2:30 in the afternoon. All of us were completely spellbound by the struggle. The king snake finally managed to get the head of the copperhead in his mouth, and it was then a matter of swallowing the copperhead, a little at a time.

As the swallowing continued, I wondered if the king snake would be absolutely exhausted and just lie there on the patio when it was over. Gradually, gradually the copperhead was disappearing; then there was only an inch or so visible. Then gone!

Immediately the king snake took off in an effortless wriggle, back and forth in a beautiful, graceful glide, as if he had not just swallowed a copperhead of his own approximate size! In no more that a minute he had crossed the patio and the flower bed, climbed the four to five foot high stone wall and disappeared into the growth on the hillside. All gone from our sight! Gone to rest and digest, I suppose.

Alys spent time talking with the children about books, music, wildlife surrounding us and many other things of interest. She drew pictures of Graham throwing snowballs at himself when, as a very small boy, there was no one else to play in the snow with him. She let Graham play with a lazy Susan that made Swiss music as it turned, and he whistled the tune until he was so tickled with what he was doing he could not pucker his lips to make a sound. Alys also shared stories of her ventures with the children so that I could enjoy them, too, and she talked with them about books they had read and adventures they had known.

Jack, the super intellect always, learned the fine points of coaching baseball and gave several years to teaching those lucky young boys of the knothole team he coached. James was fortunate enough to be a part of that team sponsored by the Hillsboro-Harding Road Exchange Club. jack taught him how to hit, to pitch, and to play the bases and how to field. The parents enjoyed the team activities as much as the boys who were a part of the team. Such happy days for all of us. James eventually made the sports page when he pitched a one-hitter in a contest for the championship at John Trotwood Moore School one hot summer's afternoon. As the pitcher's mother, I was so nervous I walked back and forth while folding the paper cup which had held my Coca Cola into a "thing" the size of a quarter before the game had ended. It is an afternoon to remember. The players, their whole families, especially the parents, are ever indebted to Jack for his time and his fine coaching of those growing boys.

* * *

October 11, 1970

Have you ever tried to stand motionless and remote from worldly surroundings - to stand apart from the struggle for existence as the moisture from the damp earth rises, creeps through the soles of your shoes and makes your feet cold! I have; and as the wind blew cool against my face partially penetrating the warmth of clothing, with it came the unexpected but inscrutable and inescapable aromas from the dark earth and the molding woods, the fragrance of mint and the pungency of sage.

Riding the morning air came the twitter of birds, the snapping of a branch, the perpetual chirping of crickets. The simple process of standing with open eyes brought realization of semi-brightness of the sun unfalteringly going about penetration of the surrounding fog. A hickory limb reverberated and swished its leafy bough as a squirrel leaped from its insecurity to the stable body of the tree trunk and scampered briskly down with reptilian grace. Two late-summer moths excitedly flittered near the last blooming flowers, and what seemed aimless activity surely had meaning that I did not grasp.

I sought to be detached, and it was pleasant; but somehow there was a sub-surface feeling that I could not stand without actually contemplating the cool, the light, the sound that came to me without my beckoning. How long could one stand thus? I seemed to lose a sense of my own reality, but something inside me fought to return, and I found myself moving back toward the door, a step at a time, muscles coming singly, then rapidly into activity. The cold brass of the handle in my hand gave way to my grasp, and I entered the familiar room ready to grapple with the reality of my responsibility.

* * *

October 30, 1970

As comfortable as the feeling of permanency that must come when the roots of a transplanted tree have found union with the new earth into which they have been set. - Comfort that comes through perfect interaction and the establishment of lines of nourishment. (Brought to mind in checking the condition of a newly planted pear tree.)

A swarm of grackles "set in upon" the magnolia tree in Jack and Alys' yard (so grandly supporting its redheaded cones) in a <u>greedy</u> attack; yet they fed gingerly and nervously as if feeding in stealth and expecting to be chased away from their "find," Some ominous air surrounded their being in the tree and contrasted (initially, sharply) with the bold glare of the sun upon the waxy green leaves. Something in the brightness distracted one's thoughts in such a way that the uneasy grackles left as if spirited away to another spot for feeding, not far, only out of sight; but their shrill chattering bespoke their presence and continued to press their intrusion upon one's attempt at peaceful thinking.

* * *

Peach Policeman

Graham came home from nursery school one day and announced that he was going to be a <u>peach policeman</u> when he grew up.

We had no earthly idea what a <u>peach</u> policeman could be, unless maybe it was his way of identifying with a "pinkish-looking" "white" policeman.

One night, some weeks later, the phone rang while we were having dinner. I answered it myself.

"This is Lt. Peach of the Nashville Police Department, Mrs. Perry. Chief Mott asked me to call you to say I'd be glad to speak to your DAR chapter."

I could hardly control my amusement! "Lt. Peach, have you been to Westminster School recently?"

"Well, yes, I have."

"I want you to know that my four-year-old son has decided to be like you. He goes around daily saying 'I want to be a <u>Peach</u> policeman when I grow up!'"

* * *

When James and Graham were in their first year at Nashville Christian School, James had a football game in the park through which the Harpeth River ran. The game lasted with the late day drizzle, and darkness had almost descended.

I spent most of the afternoon with Jan Smith, the mother of Graham's best buddy, Danny Smith. Suddenly I realized we had not seen Graham and Danny for some time. "Jan, you don't suppose they've gone down to the river do you?" Both of us jumped up at the very idea and started running toward the river.

Just as we approached the Harpeth, we saw two little boys headed toward us. There were Graham and Danny. My "heart in my throat", I asked, "You didn't contemplate going in that river did you, Graham?"

"No, Mother, I knew I didn't have the Arc of the Covenant!"

They had really learned a lot more than I knew about the Bible in first grade at NCS! Later, he told me about Moses, the Arc of the Covenant, his "people" and the Red Sea as it parted for their crossing!

* * *

We thought it was such a privilege to be able to meet a group out at the park where a Vanderbilt professor of astronomy was lecturing about constellations with a telescope available for seeing some of them. George took his first grader, Graham, who was attending a church school, to have a look. When the astronomer finished telling the story of Cassiopeia to the assembled group, Graham blurted out loudly with his great enthusiasm and his growing knowledge of <u>Bible</u> stories, "Just like a Jezebel!"

* * *

One day Martha's teacher needed to attend a meeting, so she asked me if I would come to school and teach a reading class for her in the afternoon. I was thrilled to be asked and happily went to Martha's fourth grade class to work with the children. I felt that we had a great time reading and discussing the story! Afterwards, I drove happily home and waited for Martha to return on her school bus.

When the bus arrived, I looked out of the front door and started to meet Martha. She was crying and quite angry. "What on earth is the matter, darling?"

Answer: "It's bad enough to have the <u>oldest</u> mother in the room, but you didn't have to <u>tell</u> the class how old you are!" (My age - 40.)

* * *

September 16, 1970

At forty-five, I feel like a mid-September day - - warm, sunny, at peace, but a little parched and apprehensive of the season to come. I hope to be responsive to the rest of living in the same manner as the aforesaid day, ready to be reinvented by the slightest shower or a gentle rain, to feel again like a full-summer's day even though the illusion might be ever so momentary.

There is a satisfaction and an inner feeling of gratification that transposes the inevitable changing of seasons to come into a welcome of the potential excitement.

* * *

James, upon indoctrinating himself into the use of a deodorant said, "Mother, I've put on my shirt and taken it off <u>five</u> times before I realized that the "thing" I hadn't put on was my Ban Spray Deodorant. Ban is nice, but tell me, have you ever used Right Guard?"

Age 9

* * *

One day, when she was in the 10th grade, Elizabeth came home from Hillwood High School and said rather caustically, "The Fitzhughs are <u>so</u> conceited!" There were three Fitzhugh boys in high school.

I asked, "<u>What</u> are they so conceited about?"

"Oh, they wear Weejuns (loafers)!"

"What's the difference? You wear Weejuns, too?" Mother

Elizabeth, "Oh, they <u>talk</u> about <u>theirs</u>!"

* * *

Tra la, tra la (for want of a better thought)

All the bells on earth shall ring on Christmas Day in the morning!

Nobody else but the rose bush knows

How well-paved the road to ____ is with good intentions at this season.

Why this gift is not complete, only you can guess the reason!

* * *

James -

On the subject of burglar's having cut three or four holes in the roof of Diamond Hill Plywood - "Daddy, they must have been really <u>creative</u> to bypass the burglar alarm and cut all those holes!"

* * *

James -

"When you <u>die,</u> you <u>live</u> in your <u>own special</u> way."

* * *

Jesus Green on the way back to our bus from London, a small jazzy band was seated there playing songs of Cole Porter! Fond memory, especially of the pastry I bought from a street vendor to munch on with my cup of tea.

* * *

George and I luxuriated together while watching the tennis match between Conners and the "boy from

University of Tennessee. . . Anaconda." The love and closeness of a mate are ever what it's all about!

* * *

The family across the street are celebrating with the <u>right thing</u>, as usual. We hear the popping and cracking of fireworks! They are, of course, as always, unlawful in Davidson County, but that aspect has never seemed to bother that "All American" family!. . . George began to laugh, remembering the time we let James and Graham buy some firecrackers to take to Pa Pa's house in North Carolina. We said, "You can't shoot them in Nashville because it is against the law, but we'll let you take them to North Carolina where it isn't!". . . James and Graham let go all the restraint of their emotions and set out to shoot up all of the fireworks as soon as we arrived at Castalia! They had shot a few dozen when, all of a sudden, the siren from the fire hall went off, announcing that it was twelve o'clock, midday. The horror of sheer fright was written all over the boys' faces and in their frantic haste to put up the firecrackers! They came running toward us, the siren still going off full blast. George said, "The fuzz!" And it took some high-powered explaining to get these little boys to realize that the police were not coming for them!. . . I wonder if they remember!

* * *

Is there <u>anything</u> that belies reality and reckoning with the <u>truth</u> more than watching a snowstorm from the secure, snug warmth of a house with a fire on the hearth? The snow is falling with a hushed softness that covers the earth like a blanket and enhances the surrounding trees and bushes with a feathery bloom that otherwise could never be theirs. Outside is the cold, the white; inside is the warmth, the glow; and in the heart is excitement that only comes with snow. (This is especially true of our home on Rolling Fork.)

* * *

April 19, 1971

To the Editor:

The year's at the spring this morning in the freshest, warmest and sunniest way. I couldn't help realizing, as the front door slammed and my nine year old son started enthusiastically toward the bus stop, that school will soon be out.

As I walked back through my son's room, I noted the boyish disarray. There were baseball gloves, this year's and last season's and a ball and bat. Near them was a scattering of baseball collectors' cards. An unpainted ship's model and a freshly painted rocket, ready to launch, decorated the desk, and there were various other mementos surrounding the one book, Old Yeller, partially read and lying open at page 96. My eyes quickly bypassed the rumpled bed and spotted a container filled with straw and water, hopefully growing paramecia; a microscope; a bowl of goldfish; a bowl of turtles; two unfinished rocket models and a brand new football trophy. In the lavatory just around the corner was a glass with two toothbrushes, noticeably dry for this time of morning. A wet towel on the floor and a pair of pajamas looked comfortingly "used."

As I surveyed the remnants of a weekend at home and thought of the few weeks left for going to school, I found myself praying for the patience and understanding and know-how to make the coming vacation months a safe, healthy, satisfying and glorious period of boyhood and growing up for my son. I remembered my sometime-criticism of the schools and gave thanks for all the kind help and good teaching that have been given my child. I found myself breathing a prayer for the kind of guidance that will give a parent what it takes to keep her child growing and developing during the summer into a person who will be happy and self-confident, considerate and thoughtful of others, and able to make a worthwhile contribution to the world in his lifetime.

The same thoughts and wishes are for my other children and other people's children; it just happened that my son slammed the door this morning with the most verve, and the evidences of his good weekend were the most poignant and widely scattered. All of this had simply brought to mind the real joy and challenge of parenthood as a complement to this gorgeous spring morning.

Mrs. George Perry, Jr.

* * *

Nov. 18

The full-leafed maple stood confident and grand in spite of the hint of yellow that was beginning to betray its green leaves. Suddenly one day it boasted in full sunlight a pure and billowing cloud of golden fullness which seemed to brag of health and stability that willows and hickories had let go some days earlier when their leaves had browned, dried and fallen to the ground.

Then in the early morning sun appeared beneath the maple a carpet of yellow leaves, and subsequently and as if by true stealth in the nighttime, the carpet grew and piled higher. At first the fullness of the tree belied its loss, then the brown twigs of branches began to show. With the coming of a dark and cold morning, the grand maple suddenly showed its age and the reality of the advancing seasons. The remaining leaves were few, and their brightness of the last week had turned to ochre.

The thin leaves, the almost bare tree, and the darkness of the sky mixed with penetrating dampness to make one suspect that snow was in the offing and winter a near reality.

I walked toward the carpet of maple leaves, now not so yellow and seeming in the grayness of the day to be giving way to an ashen white; but as I approached, I noticed a heretofore-undetected color. The latest ochre-fallen leaves were tinged as if by orange, and they lay there in unsuspected warmth, undetermined thickness, and closeness protective of the damp earth and cold bricks. I walked through with a mixture of emotion and appreciation of their silence as it seemed to arise to meet my steps.

* * *

May 3, 1984

Dear Graham has said for some time that he has his very own relationship with God. It does not necessarily fit into anyone else's theology, especially that of the Baptists and members of the church of Christ, the people with whom he has been in most contact during his life here in the Bible Belt. . .

Last night I overheard him talking to Rob. "I have always subscribed to what I call 'The Trainset Philosophy of God.' Don't you?" he asked.

Obviously having been asked to verbalize on the subject, he continued, "Well, have you ever built a layout for a train set. . . trees and building and people and trains and stations and all that? I have built some elaborate ones, and when I was through, I just sat there on the floor beside it, and I wished and imagined that all of those things would come to life. . . that those people would take off doing things their own way while I sat and watched. Then I could have stepped in at any moment, but I didn't want to. I wanted to see what they would do for themselves. . . let them make their own mistakes and their own triumphs. . . I just sat there and loved them and believed they could do it!. . . I didn't try to interfere in my moments of imagining that they were real. I just wanted to see them do it themselves. . . Well, that's sort of the way I look at God. . . He wants us to do things for ourselves. . . He has given us everything to

A Fire on the Hearth

work with. . . and that's sort of what I call my 'Trainset Philosophy of God.'"

* * *

Once there was a little boy named Georgia.

He had a pleasant little face with two big dimples, a smiling mouth that turned up at the corners, two bright blue eyes, and a wisp of hair that stood right up on the crown of his head. Graham!

* * *

March 9, 1972

Some of life's "little boy" surprises:

A first grader coming home after school (wearing his best white-knit shirt) with his arm around a rusting tin can pressing against his fat tummy. Water, muddy and rusty, splashes out with each step, and he stops periodically, thrusts in an arm up to and beyond his coat cuff, to pull out a tremendous crayfish to show to curious children.

4:45 in the afternoon finds cabinet doors open in the kitchen, a fresh loaf of bread draped across the cabinet spilling white slices onto the floor. The nearby table has an open, smeared jar of grape jelly, a silver butter spreader and a "best" tea spoon - - and - - a mouse trap!

Carpet of Yellow Leaves

* * *

<u>My favorite compliments</u>

"Mrs. J. has a way of bringing out the best that there is in every child."

Logan Harding

Principal

Patrick Copeland School

* * *

"You have the best hand in the world with salt and pepper."

Al

* * *

"You're certainly <u>not</u> the most beautiful girl in the world, but <u>sometimes</u> you make me think you are."

Al

* * *

"Mrs. Perry, there's not a 'store boughten' thing about you (and your home and family)"

Mrs. R. D. Tankersley

"I love you because your mouth turns up at the corners when you smile."

Daddy

After Christmas

"Mom, do you realize that each one of us children has a 'one on one' relationship with you. You make each one of us feel special in his own way. That's why we relate to you better than we do each other."

Graham

Sunset on Our Ridge

- Like having watched the sun setting on the far side of a wooded hill in winter
Dark trees - foreboding sentinels, the stark victims of their command
Steadfast in their appointed guard
A relentless foreground for a fading brilliance and a waning glory.

George spent evening after evening sitting on the sofa with Graham going through the furniture book, looking especially at clocks. This was the period preceding his third year. As we held him in arm in an antique shop (Sarah Green's) in Raleigh that summer, he spied a barometer on the wall. He absolutely shocked Sarah Green when he (baby that he was) suddenly pointed to the barometer and with wild enthusiasm shouted, "Look, it's a <u>Regency</u> clock!"

Also, while taking a walk with me up the street where the area is very wooded, he spied a very straight, tall poplar tree. It had a huge round burl near the top-middle section. He suddenly pointed to it and said, "Look, there's a David Rittenhouse!" I daresay not many three year olds are familiar with David Rittenhouse clocks! (Especially enough to make that association.)

* * *

Spelling

Martha

October 15

B 1. soldiers

vegetables

2. pond

ponds

3. circuses

inches

4. patches

   touches

5. grapes

   bananas

   roots

   articles

   sports

6. ba nan a

   mem bers

7. spears

   blossoms

   charaters

8. avenue

   ashes

* * *

Feb. 1975

Mother: "Tell Miss Alys that you <u>did</u> comb your hair,
but it's still sticking up in all directions."

Graham: "I <u>know</u>. My hair just <u>won't</u> obey!"

* * *

Liz: "I think Gerald Ford is much like General
Rommel. I think he's basically a good man, but I think
he's being <u>used</u> as a front for other people."

* * *

Scene: Dinner table with present Mother, Father, two

boys, aged eleven and seven, and a fifteen-year-old daughter.

Mother: "All right , boys, keep your food on your plate, and don't eat so fast. I abhor bad table manners. Do you know what I mean by that?"

Father: "To abhor means to find despicable. Now do you understand?"

Eleven-year-old boy: "Well, yes, but that's not what the abhor I know about means!"   (James)

September 25, 1972

* * *

My Autobiography

My name is James Jennings. I was born in Greensboro, North Carolina on June 23, 1961. I am 5 feet 2 inches tall, weigh 104 pounds.

My mother's name is Charlotte B. Perry. She is very understandable and likes to participate in patriotic clubs such as the Daughters of the American Revolution, Daughters of the American Colonists and the Colonial Dames. She is an ex-Youth Symphony Mother. I have a step-father whose name is George Graham Perry, Jr. Ret. Col. in Army Res. He is a WWII veteran and works at Diamond Hill Plywood Company. I have one brother and two sisters. My brother's name is Graham Perry III. He is eight years old and is in third grade. Elizabeth Jennings, my older sister, is 19 and is a Junior at Western Kentucky University. Martha Jennings, my youngest sister, is 17 and is a Junior at Hillwood. We live at 6604 Rolling Fork Dr.

Right now I attend Nashville Christian School and am in seventh grade.

* * *

An unequivocal observation upon nature's (life's) system of checks and balances this morning is that of necessity of <u>conformity</u> to the reasonable in order to escape a certain amount of inevitable <u>penalty</u>.

The thought involved my laughing at myself as I "scraped the bowl" after making a batch of <u>double</u> fudge brownies. In refusing to give in to my craving desire to "lick the bowl" I saw myself as middle-aged and facing a sure penalty of overindulgence no matter <u>how</u> tempting the morsel. I longed for one of my children to enjoy the bowl scraping, as children are always entitled to in our middle-class homes (a child-mother mutual joy).

The thought occurred to me that a child is denied the position and competence to decide <u>when</u> to make cakes and how to make cakes; otherwise, he would be subject to the temptation of overindulgence, perhaps beyond his level of development. The grown-up, though also tempted (and sorely), has hopefully developed a realization of that which would serve his own good end. Maturity has its temptations, but it is blessed by the power of recognition, of contemplation beyond the moment, and the built-in mechanism of restraint when it is seen as the best solution.

Growing older is not really too bad at all when savored! In fact it feels much like a reward for having persevered!

Tra la!

Feb. 25, 1972

* * *

September 27

Imagine a Nashville Christian pep rally with 287 students plus teachers assembled to generate enthusiasm for the first varsity football game in the history of the new school. James, as a member of the junior varsity, must have been a symbol of real pride to his younger brother, Graham, aged seven. All of a sudden Graham raised his hand from a row near the front. The principal, Mr. Owen, noticed, and said, "Brother Graham has something he wants to say."

Graham stood up, smiled, flexed his muscles and proudly said to the assembly, "If you still have a football team when I get big enough, I'm going to be on it, and I'm really going to <u>fight</u>! I'm going to be a blocker!" . . . To which the whole assembly applauded enthusiastically, long and loud, while mirthfully appreciating the simplicity and spontaneity of the second grader.

James said later, "They all laughed and applauded and liked what Graham said, but I was really embarrassed. Everyone said, 'Is he your brother?'" . . . James gave the impression that it was al right for Graham to do that, but . . . he really didn't know whether or not he liked it!

The thrill of the day was when Graham Perry finally met Anthony, the black student who plays football. He said, "I said, 'Hi, Anthony', and he said, "'hi, Jennings.'" What a thrill!

* * *

January 9

Graham

Mom, I swear I saw the other side of the moon. . . the one that's dark! . . . On a nearly-dark day when there was a snow on the ground and the one-quarter moon obviously was part of a complete circle.

* * *

Upon "picking out" Bach . . . "Jesu, Joy of Man's Desiring" . . . "Wouldn't that be great played on the bagpipes?" Graham

* * *

Valentine's Day 1973 . . .

First thing in A.M.

Graham gave valentines just alike to Daddy, James, and the dog, Cub. Daddy asked him how they all rated having exactly the same kind of valentine to which he replied, "Cause they were the only ones I had left!"

Graham picked a valentine with an elephant on it to give to the tiniest girl in the room, Lisa, and he said, "I picked the elephant because I wanted Lisa to know how it feels to be BIG!"

James's basketball practice was cancelled so we (Graham, James, and I) went to see Mrs. Tankersley. Graham carried her the candy hearts he received at the school party which Mrs. Wells, Mrs. Allen and I gave them, and James carried her a nosegay which I made out of yellow and white daisies. She was so thrilled to see us. The best thing I can offer my children in life is to share themselves with other people and to be loved in return. All of them seem at this stage of the game to have caught on. Graham stood his ground firmly with Mrs. Tankersley and said, "I love Mrs. Rudy, but I still love you, too, Mrs. Tankersley!"

We were so thrilled to have a free afternoon that we made a family valentine for the Venables next door and forgot all about James's music lesson. The treat of our lives is to have a few free moments at home. We completely forget everything else when we have a chance to be here!

George came in the door at five-thirty, and I asked him if he picked James up. He looked blank and said, "From where?" I answered, "From music, of course!". . . To which he admitted that he had completely forgotten, and we gleefully admitted that we had completely forgotten, too! . . . And we had a completely happy evening although we couldn't get Liz on the phone in Bowling Green and George had to go to choir practice.

* * *

No story of our lives on Rolling Fork would be complete without the mention of our dear, honored friend, Jeanette. It was she who taught the children so many things: how to hunt, how to revere Indian relics and the value of archaeology, how to learn from baseball and football and enjoy them for a lifetime. She was instrumental in building Graham's love for

Native American lore and history as well as coin and stamp collecting. She taught James the ethics of the woods and the joy of the hunting world. Because Jeanette took her, Martha Sills was able to return to Dallas and the cotton Bowl, which she had longed to do since our sudden departure when she was four years old. Jeanette also treated Martha and James to a World Series game in Cincinnati when Pete Rose was at his zenith. Every one of us loved and admired and respected Jeanette. She made life so much more interesting for all of us. Our love continues - always. She is a legend to be handed down by my children to their children.

* * *

Another interesting sidelight as to our development to date was Martha's absolute disbelief, not that the men returning as prisoners of war after six to seven years in Viet Nam had been without food American style, love or home, but that they <u>hadn't</u> been able to <u>spend any money or go shopping</u> in the length of time! Ha!

* * *

September

Too many joys of parenthood are sudden, are there, and are gone. Lest I forget . . . one of my most joyful and appreciated compliments came from James, whom I had been picking up after a hot two hours of football practice at four every day. This particular day he was supposed to wait an extra thirty minutes for his daddy to pick him up, and he dreaded it! When I showed up at the usual time instead, he was obviously pleased as he approached the car. When he opened the door and saw a bottle of Gatorade waiting on the seat beside me in its usual place, he exclaimed, "Gee, Mom, you sure are faithful. . . You'd make a good dog!"

* * *

Graham, in the early morning hours, when he couldn't sleep, was thinking hopefully ahead to Christmas. He said, "I certainly hope we have snow for Christmas!" He mused a moment or two; then in absolute innocence he asked plaintively, "Mom, is <u>God</u> or <u>Santa Claus</u> responsible for getting snow?"

* * *

October

Two bittersweet-orange branches of hawthorn berries arched and swayed gently down toward the slope of the hillside, and three feet above them, in equal grace and curve, were September-yellow goldenrod, blooming their seasonal and just-right heads. For days I looked and enjoyed their touch of color against the fading and drying green of the woods. Somehow the distance separating their color was a mite too great and I hoped that next season an added branch of berries or an extra bit of goldenrod might fill the space that caused a gap to the artistic eye. Then, one morning I cast a glance at the hillside and the purple-blue of a wild New England aster was there, filling in the space, not boldly, but rightly. Before this, I had not any prescience of its being. Its tough, woody stems and sparse foliage are hardly discernible from so great a distance; yet it had been there all along, and I had not noticed. . . What connection is there, if any, between my desire to surfeit the spot with color and the hand that put it there? Can wishing make it so, or is there some unseen force that makes things right for the man who longs or hopes or plans?

* * *

October 1974

On passing a mailbox with a white towel tied to it, I said "Graham, it looks as if they're giving up back there. Did you see that white flag?"

He rode along solemnly for a few seconds, then said, "Oh, I think they're celebrating the Passover. I think I saw a little <u>blood</u>."

* * *

Written by James, aged 14, when at twenty minutes until nine o'clock on Sunday night he remembered he had to do a paper on "Procrastination". . .

"The worst thing that a man can do is procrastinate. Procrastination never has done and never will do anybody any good. If a man has put something off until the latest possible date, he cannot possibly do a good job on that thing. He would have too much pressure on him and more than likely ~~he would~~ his mind would be ~~thinking about what he will be doing after the job is finished~~ on something else. Under these circumstances, who could do ~~service~~ a job well? Whatever the person did get done would be done only halfway because of the lack of time and the lack of concentration. To get something done right, a person has to do it before the last minute.

Let us pretend that someone has put ~~something~~ a thing off ~~so that he can~~ in order to enjoy ~~another thing at the present time in the immediate future~~ something else. Could this person really enjoy himself? It is not likely. ~~Who~~ No one could possibly enjoy himself with an unpleasant task hanging over his head. His conscience would ~~have~~ force him to feel guilty.

What good does procrastination do? The extra time produced is not thoroughly enjoyed, and jobs to be done are done badly. If procrastination does no good, why do all men do it? ~~No one, not even you the reader, can answer that.~~ You, the reader, must answer that for yourself."

* * *

February 1975

Graham came out to get in the car when school was over, arms loaded with books, and kicked at the door impatiently. I leaned over and pulled the handle down to let him in. As he threw his books on the seat, he looked at me and asked breathlessly, "Mom, what are 'the facts of life'? Everybody in the class knows except me and Donnie!"

I mused for a second, looking for the right response, but he demanded again, "What are 'the facts of life'?"

I said, "I suppose you're talking about where babies come from."

"Oh, is that what they're talking about?"

Imagine the amusement on the part of Martha and Elizabeth at the blatant, innocent way he announced to us the colloquial words he had learned for committing the "facts of life." He said, <u>Rachel</u> says it means _____."

* * *

February 13

To dispel the gloom of a cold, nearly-rainy day:

- from the window while washing dishes, I can see a row of yellow, early buttercups lining the woods' edge. On the bare limbs of the peach tree, near the stone walk, perch simultaneously a male cardinal, a blue jay, and a wine-dipped purple finch. At the same time, a redheaded flicker is feeding from the feeder as he holds tenaciously onto it from its bottom. Unbelievable display of nature's vivid colors! It is so exciting to live near the woods!

* * *

1975

In January of his 9th year, Graham was riding along beside me when he said, "Mom, don't you wish there weren't any such thing as <u>sin</u>?"

As always, trying to lighten his approach to such subjects, I said, "Well - it depends what you mean by <u>sin</u>."

He said, "Oh, <u>you</u> know. Adam and Eve started sin - or maybe it was the Devil. . . Anyway (thoughtfully) I guess Adam and Eve weren't <u>really</u> responsible for their sin like we are. After all, they were the <u>first</u> people and they really weren't <u>developed</u> like we are!"

* * *

August 19, 1975

Graham got a trumpet for his 10th birthday. Before his second lesson from Mike Williams, he had "picked out" "When the Saints Go Marching In," much to Mike's amazement.

The lady who sold him the trumpet said as she took it out of the wrapper, "Now this instrument has never been out of the case before. Any scratches and marks to be put on it will be the ones <u>you</u> make." Two weeks later, in the enthusiasm of marching down the hall while playing "The Saints" he ran into the door knob of the bathroom door, it being just the right height to fit into the oncoming trumpet. There was a momentary horror on Graham's face, but fortunately there were no marks! What pleasure he has had with the instrument!

On the discovery of a rat in my herb garden outside the window, George and Graham went out to try to kill him. George was armed with a shovel; Graham went trumpet in hand. I kept hearing Graham exclaim, "There he is, Daddy." Finally, he began to improvise "The Charge." I couldn't bear to watch as the proceedings went on. "There he is!" Then alternating came Graham's rendition of "The Charge." After a few minutes I heard, very solemnly, Graham playing (improvised on the spot) "Taps." The outcome was evident. Cub, the dog, had captured the rat!

About two months later I asked Graham if he didn't want to practice the trumpet. Came a voice from the living room, "I <u>am</u> going to practice. After all a <u>trumpet is a man's best friend</u>!"

Graham is much concerned about handing down his coin collection, etc., to <u>his</u> children. He keeps talking about when he is a father!

This morning he said, "Mother, I keep wondering how I'm going to be a father. I don't know <u>anything</u> about <u>how</u> I'm going to be a father. What I mean is, I don't know what <u>I'm</u> supposed to do to be a father!"

Guessing, naturally, that he didn't know <u>his</u> side of "the facts of life," I said, "Well, I could tell you, but it will be such a <u>long</u> time before you need to know, do you suppose you could <u>wait</u> a while?"

He answered, with a sheepish grin, "Yes, I can wait."

Then, as I turned to leave the room, he said, "I can wait until <u>tomorrow</u>!"

Having decided "on his own" to go out for the football team, Graham went proudly and hopefully out to Nashville Christian School to the first practice the morning of August 14. He was fitted with helmet, equipment, and was armed with the usual papers to fill out.

At five o'clock I took him back to school to get on the bus to go out to the field for the first session. He was terribly out of shape physically, having suffered much all summer with allergies.

My fears materialized when George came in just before dinner with Graham. He exploded, "It was just as bad as I thought!" I <u>couldn't</u> keep up! I was thirsty and I couldn't breathe and I got too tired, etc.!"

Later in the evening he was still complaining, "I didn't even like to ride the bus! It was bumpy and hot!"

I said, "Graham, <u>stop</u> complaining. Let's face it; you weren't cut out for football!"

He looked up at me, the most knowing, adorable grin on his face. "Now, Mother, don't you remember the story about the fox and the grapes?"

We had a good chuckle together, and, I suppose, that has ended Graham's football career!

Alys reminded me today of the time when Graham was three that he consoled James. The sun was going down and James was lamenting the fact that it was disappearing for the day.

Graham said, "<u>Don't</u> worry, James, it will be back tomorrow when the earth turns!"

* * *

Elizabeth is going back to school at Belmont. I do pray that she will meet a few wonderful people who will mean a lot to her. She is basically so sweet and wants to see the good side of people. So many people have disappointed her. She is a good thinker, far more practical in mind than is usually exemplified at her age. She, like George, can <u>see through things</u> and come to conclusions about them. I am so proud of the progress she has made for herself in this past year at the bank, in spite of health difficulties that have plagued her. She reminds me of Granny Boone and could be equally as strong in character.

* * *

Martha Sills came home from Hillwood High School one day and said very seriously, "Mother, there is something I want to ask you, but I don't know whether I should."

"Go ahead and ask me. If I know the answer, I'll tell you."

"Well - - what does it mean when they say Merrill Lynch is bullish on America?"

* * *

When Martha Sills made a first trip to Spain while in high school, she was away for 11 days. Other mothers were getting postcards and letters from their children. Every day I went down to my mailbox, hoping I'd hear from Martha. Nothing! Not a word.

We were having an early supper before going to the airport to meet our returning students when the phone rang. It was a collect call from Martha Sills in Philadelphia. "I'm back, Mother!"

"Why didn't you write me a single card? I was worried! Are you all right?"

"Oh, yes! I had a good time, but the stamps cost nearly twice as much as they do here, so I decided to save my money!

Would that her thriftiness could continue to some extent! She loves to shop!

* * *

August 18, 1975

Martha Sills left this morning for Samford University. I can hardly believe that that soft, dear, wonderful child has come to the stage in life when she must grow up (has really matured into a very grown-up lady) and grow away from us. What a wonderful young lady I have sent them!

* * *

One night when we were eating dinner after Martha Sills had gone to Samford, the phone rang, and she breathlessly said, "Well tonight I have finally won my first <u>religious</u> argument. I said, 'There are two things from the <u>Bible</u> my mother always taught us. ' Judge not that you be not judged' and 'This above all, to thine own self be true!'"

"Well, dear, I'm certainly glad you remembered those things, even if one is from Shakespeare instead of the Bible!"

* * *

Fall 1975

James's comment upon first being served cooked turnips - "Where's the <u>blood</u>?"

I am always telling them, "You can't get blood out of a turnip." That is - when they ask me for <u>money</u>."

* * *

Martha's notes . . . New Testament 7-1-76

Cash check

Buy fingernail polish

Check dates played tennis

Test Wed. 88-100

2nd Coming of Christ

Anticipation is to life what salt is to food

* * *

Three weeks before Valentine's Day when James was fourteen he came into the house with a small heart-shaped, fancy box of chocolates he had bought with the remainder of the $5.00 he had borrowed from George. Everyone wanted to know "who it was for." He grinned sheepishly and said, "It's for my girl."

The Friday before Valentine's Day I was vacuuming underneath his bed and ran into an obstacle the vacuum wouldn't pick up. I bent down to retrieve it . . . there it was . . . an empty heart-shaped box!

I was really encouraged to know that a fourteen-year-old boy's weakness was still chocolates in preference to girls!

* * *

Friday night, January 16, 1976, found our woods and hills at 6604 Rolling Fork Drive blanketed with a light snowfall and lighted by a full moon. No words are yet fashioned that would be adequate for describing the beauty, the quiet, the peace, the feeling that poured over and through one in looking out into the night. The moon was absolutely round, its circumference a flowing ring, golden, but of a silvered hue, if that be possible. The brightness had a cold look, so unlike the orange-gold of a harvest moon. A silvered light made every object visible as if by day, except that each one bore behind it a shadow, and the whole scene was one of foreboding. Things seemed real, but unreal; and the whole expanse was scattered with brilliant, sparkling diamonds. Each curled brown leaf was filled with soft snow; each cold, dark limb was piled high with the same feather-like whiteness. The radiating bits of the spectrum in diamond-like glittering seemed to have been scattered by the hand of a masterful farmer who had sown his grain with one majestic sweep. There they lay in the stillness of the night, seeming to be made up of pure, unadulterated potential energy. In their simply lying there, they seemed to leap up to penetrate the night with atom-splitting excitement. In the moonlight they sparkled, glistened, shone!

One heartwarming bit of knowledge had come to us in the early twilight. As the grayness of the cloudy afternoon began to deepen into darkness, the whirling snowflakes came down larger and faster. The wind blew some, and it was obvious that this evening we'd all want to share a family fire in the den fireplace. I asked James to bring in a few armfuls of wood so Daddy wouldn't have to go out again in the cold when he returned from his hard day's work. The lure of a warm, cozy evening must have been the background for an eager willingness to do the job; so, with the boundless energy and ever-ready curiosity of a fourteen-year-old boy, he went out the back door toward the woodpile at the edge of the trees. As he passed the bluebird box, standing alone on its four-foot post in the creeping night, he pulled the top off and gave an aimless peep in just to have something extra to do, a boyish move to make. To his surprise, there, huddled together inside were five full-grown bluebirds, three grayish females and two males, their color shouting back their blueness, even into the cold, grey late afternoon.

He put the top back on the box immediately, this time with more calculated thought, headed quickly for the wood pile, and picked up an armful of three-foot logs. As he opened the door to the house, sniffing back the cold in short breaths of excitement, he told me what he had found.

Now, one human failing of the well-fed, thinking, middle-class American is that he can never seem to let

Snow in the Moonlight

"well enough" alone! Anything good can surely be made a little better, even a simple circumstance already in the powerful hands of the natural laws of the woods. Our hearts "went out" to those wonderful little blue feathered treasures nestled, no doubt quite comfortably, in the little brown box on the post, protected from the present ferocity of the elements, out of the reach of their arch enemies, the cat and the blue jay. The post was too straight for climbing; the hole in the box was too small for the jay's bullying and dominating way. We had but to sit inside by the roaring fire on the hearth and be filled with the good cheer of knowing our box housed five of the most coveted tenants from the birds of the wood. The path of the bluebird's enemies at this moment certainly led in other directions, and their concerns must have been for a shelter of their own, wherever it may have been! Alas!

My motherly instincts kindled, and no doubt heightened by the good circumstances of my own brood at the moment, I called to Graham who actually claimed the bluebirds' box as his own property. Uncle Mac had built it for him and had given it to him with specific information about these wonderful, rare little creatures. "Graham," I said, "go to the basement, get a clean board, and take it outside near the bluebird house. Fill it with sunflower seeds, and they will be able to find some food if it doesn't snow too deep."

With gladsome heart and willing hands, the ten-year-old boy fashioned an eating place for the birds, to be in readiness on the cold, frozen morning we expected to follow. Mission accomplished, we all went about our business of enjoying the kind of evening just made for togetherness and the blessings of knowing the "bosom" of a family.

Having had the "enough-sleep" surfeit of middle age, I was awake at two o'clock a.m. With the household asleep, children breathing deeply, Daddy snoring, I crept through the darkened house, peering outside as I went, at the magic of the cold, moonlighted night. As I stood at the large glass window in the den staring at the wonder of the out-of-doors, I thought of the bluebirds huddled in the box. They seemed a treasure of the heart, and I was happy in a way that complemented my love for my sleeping family. Our larder was full; tomorrow morning there would be bacon, eggs, toast, orange juice, homemade jelly . . . a feast for them. On the clean pine board underneath the light covering of snow lay a feast for the bluebirds. Our thoughtfulness had made it possible; and that was good.

The light of dawn had hardly dispersed the aura of the moonlighted night when the frail peeps of the bird world could be heard, though barely audible and without their usual gusto. I put fresh seed on the back porch feeder, and looked toward the plank we had prepared for the little blue-feathered friends. A brazen, giant blue jay swept down for a seed. He flew boldly back to the maple tree and sat confidently there removing the kernel from the sunflower husk. With a jet-like swoop another jay had attacked the stake. Back and forth they went, time and again, over and over they came, devouring the seed, while the bluebirds still huddled in the box. Our friends were hemmed in, confined to their bit of safety while their enemies swooped back and forth outside, invading their territory, and making their escape impossible. I wondered how many seed we had so generously spread on the board there, how long the jays would feast, but most of all, whether or not the bluebirds would seek another cover as soon as possible and vacate the house we'd hoped <u>so long</u> to have them inhabit.

We couldn't take the seeds back without causing a greater disturbance! Could we think of a better way to help our friends? Should we let well enough "be" and leave the welfare of the bluebirds up to their own ingenuity and their successful exploration of their own habitat?

We decided to leave them alone to trust their survival to the nature that had nurtured them. It has been far more rewarding to stand at the frosted window since then, seeing them only occasionally as they ventured out, one at a time to find the sustenance that they need to take them into spring. We can't, however, resist building a new bluebird box or two. We have a pattern, and we'd like very much to have several families on our lot this season. We can't suppress the desire to help a little, and to hope a lot!

* * *

May 30

After the end of a coolish, gentle rain, the sun came out as stealthily as the rains had begun, and the whole day seemed warm and warming in a steaming hover. There was all-over heating as the sunshine seemed to penetrate and bear down until the earth had drunken its fill and expulsed its rays through the recently soaked topsoil with a gentle, pleasant, soul-soothing steam. It was a process no doubt not meant to be seen; but to one experiencing the May morning it was almost visible. Steam rose in little undulating spirals glistening in slivers of red and blue and violet of the spectrum.

A cautious little chipmunk crept along the stone wall, pausing, with his back hunched momentarily, to sniff around in the scattered petals of the yellow jasmine that had fallen with the rain in the night. Over its head the refreshed and still-vibrant branches waved breezily about, giving way to the weight of a bumble bee that searched without heed into first one small yellow flower, then another, with no care that they simply would not support his weight. His attack was vigorous, being sustained for the slightest of an instant; the branch swinging back into place, the bee buzzed endlessly on, his mission being one to which he was predestined, his industry showing neither boredom nor joy. A change of seasons must come in order to slow down his buzzing fury. The chipmunk elongated his brown, striped and furry body as he reached forth toward the treasure he sought. Then he sat upright holding a sunflower seed in two tiny paws, and his nibbling was furious while his jaws began to bulge with the food he was storing.

Although the garden had been planned, the seeds of the flowers having been chosen from memories of

past delights and from packages too brightly
advertising their wares, the actual effect of the
assorted blossoms and the genuine sight of their
blatant color could not have been foreseen as
experienced. The hollyhocks stood tall, a bit too tall,
their flowers bursting boldly and beautifully red into
sight about midway the leafy stalks. The blooms
graduated in size until they melded into large buds,
more buds, more and more buds, until they decreased
in size and decreased in size and grew closer and
closer and then they ended thinly and definitely and
abruptly and made the background and blue of the
sky seem to be their very own!

Here was a bit of bright blue of the ragged robin;
there nestled the bold yellow face of a single, yellow
daisy; and as hastily as the eye could wander along
the borders it picked up bits of orange and lavender,
pale pink and blue, and numerous hues of color
nestled in and out among the foliage that supported
them and gave them their backdrop.

One did not have to look skyward to know the
clouds. They were there, cumulous and feathery,
sweeping gently along with the breeze, giving proof of
their being as they cast occasional shadow on the

grass and momentarily darkened the green of the hillside.

* * *

March 12, 1976

Today my hourglass is turned over! I am fifty!

The thoughts filled with the normal pressure and rush of grains of sand in a full glass, seeking to find the smooth path of least resistance toward a final resting place; but, even that, I realize, is the excitement of which this wonderful life is made. It is my hope on this day, and in lieu of this fact, that in the course of time all of my sands will find the passage as smooth and freely-flowing as can mark the hours so that the final gush of life will come with the excitement of *joie de vie* that heralds the reward of a well-earned rest.

I shall never <u>want</u> to go, and I will probably cling to the sloping glass in the final moments with all the friction a well-worn grain of sand can possibly muster against the smooth icy glass of reality; but the prospects of lying at last in peace with all things seems hallowed, beautiful, and full of satisfaction . . . and of course . . . should there be another turning of the glass, a prospect long contemplated by mankind, I shall welcome with hope and vigor the opportunity to live and love again.

My husband and my children are the essence of my life. I hope they can know my love for them.

Today is full of excitement. March is taking on the garment which indicates that it could go out like the proverbial lion. It began with a cold rain, the winds gusting. As of this moment the rain has ceased to an occasional few misty drops, and the winds are giving the new green leaves their virginal blow as old, broken limbs swing eerily in their wake. Dark, purple-gray clouds are massed behind the hills to the north, but in the southwest there is the distinct possibility that the sun will come shining through at any moment. The fuchsia of redbud is beginning to paint the brown woods in new tones that spell life to spring. Tender early leafing trees billow here and there among them, giving a cumulus cloud-like presentation of new color, and I expect to awaken some morning to find that the stark reality of the trees in the woods will be hidden by the green foliage for months to come. It is then that the cardinals and bluebirds will not appear so startling in color, but they will go about their business of bringing up their families in the secluded shade of the forest, mostly unseen by the human eye, but evident to the ear. Birdsong will mark out territorial rights among the fowl, and their singing will delight us all, making us stop to listen.

March is not my favorite month. It has much that is too disquieting; but its lion-lamb quality is fraught with possibility... and nothing means so much to the life of man. "Hope springs eternal in the human breast" and makes one accelerate his breathing and quicken his pace.

Let's see the last of which this life is made!

* * *

January 16

As is the way with many of the "good things in life" one must develop a taste for such things as martinis, oysters, turnip greens, Shostakovich, Bach, etc. My love affair with handmade quilts was in the making for a long time, and I find myself embracing it with an enthusiasm that leaves me breathless with anxiety that I will never be able to make all the quilts that I see in lovely books and in museums.

Today is a perfect day for being engrossed in quilting and dreams of those which <u>could</u> be made. I have spent the morning looking at the gorgeous "Star and Feather" covered book Elizabeth gave me called <u>America's Quilts and Coverlets</u> by Safford and Bishop.

Outside the soft snow was first falling, then swirling, and the birds swooped down on the feeder in myriad numbers, greedily eating the sunflower seeds which would give them the stamina to ward off the freezing winds of the long, dark winter's night ahead. The top of every leaf, limb and stone wall was puffed popcorn-high with the accumulating snow. The thousands of stark, brown trees had become visible, distinguishable individuals against a background of white, and here and there on curved swaying branches cardinals, purple finches, towhees, and blue jays added their splash of bright color to the landscape like the bright birds, flowers and fruit sprouting from an appliquéd quilt. I spent an hour browsing through the book, my feeling of breathless excitement coming from the intricate work of the hundreds of women and girls who had spent so many endless hours of stitching to make these monuments to home-sewn beauty! It is unreal to think of the thousands of times they must have pricked their fingers with a needle, squinted their eyes to make a more perfect stitch, or left their dedicated work to stir a pot of soup or answer the call of a needful child. Quilts are not just bright patterns

The Fuchsia of Redbud

of intricate design, hand-sewn, and made for show. Quilts represent an idea, a dream, a desire to create, to accomplish, a determination to finish a project started, a self control that can only bring joy in a task completed. Quilting, as much as any task, is the result of a goal well thought out, with the hope of beauty and some measure of comfort and usefulness to be attained. One has to quilt a sizable project herself to realize its character-testing and developing qualities.

The first time I ever remember having noticed a bed quilt as a young child was in my Grandmother Braswell's home. She had eight living children; two more who had died in infancy. Making of cover was, of course, a necessary part of her life for years. In a separate building in the side-yard was a bedroom which had been erected as the children grew older and needed more sleeping space. There were two of these separate houses, in fact, referred to as "offices." Large trunks and blanket chests were in the office nearest the main dwelling, and I remember going with "the ladies" on many a Sunday afternoon, when, for entertainment, the visitors were invited to go and see "Miss Pattie's quilts." So, while the men sat in hickory chairs on the front porch, their feet propped on the

Victorian railing, talking of crops, world situations, farm goings on, and perhaps politics and religion, the ladies were off to find some thing of beauty in the flower garden or in the trunks which held Granny's quilts.

Some of the quilts were merely dull and utilitarian, but there were also those that proudly exhibited red and blue Pennsylvania Dutch tulips on a background of white, the "Tree of Life," the "North Carolina Lily," little girls in sun bonnets, log cabins, stars, and any number of patchwork squares sewn together with random design from whatever cloth had been available, perhaps a child's dress or shirt outgrown, but too full of good material and memories to be discarded. People always "oo-ed" and "ahh-ed" and declared which one was their favorite as my grandmother pulled them, one by amazing one, from the trunk and unfolded them for exhibition. Being a very plain looking person, unnoticeable as to personality, hard-working and off the beaten path as far as the mainstream of life was concerned, she must have realized a great deal of personal satisfaction in having her handiwork the center of attraction and the object of admiration; perhaps viewing them was mixed with a bit of envy in some cases. She was a very generous person, and often gave a quilt to someone, perhaps a married daughter or a new daughter-in-law, or a preacher's wife.

I have spent many a snowy afternoon taking a warm, cozy nap under one of Granny's quilts. I have made many a playhouse underneath one of them spread over chairs and small tables to make a sanctuary from the grownups and a house of my own for my dolls. The particular quilt I am engaged in trying to copy today is the red and blue tulip pattern on a white background, which seemed to warm me most in my childhood and live on in my memory. I still have the original one that Granny made. It is of an odd size for today because it was made for an old-fashioned three-quarter bed. The colors are dull with the softness which takes away original brilliance and lends itself to the tranquility of age, and there are holes, both worn and torn. Once it was even used by my father to wrap up dry tobacco and keep it "in order" (the moisture in). Quilts often were relegated to that place in country life when they had become worn and begun to look shabby. I retrieved this one from such a fate, brought it home to Nashville and employed it as a cover for my afternoon naps last winter. For the last year I have worked "off and on" on the one which I hope to be its replacement. My work is neither as good nor as charming, but it is my effort to preserve a thing of beauty made by my grandmother whose heart was filled with a love of things she thought pretty, those which gave her dull existence a lift from the drudgery at hand. She also wrote poetry, being a lover of beautiful words and thoughts. Perhaps some of her poetic writings were conceived as she sat tranquilly working on a quilt, pricking her fingers with the needle, her mind filling with and sorting out the essences of life.

* * *

April 22

The absolutely bold, forthright face of the daisy extrapolates its beauty and reaches from its perennial border onto my heart and soul. I don't love any growing thing more than that white-petaled, golden-centered flower with its "love me, love me not" truthfulness.

* * *

Graham said this week, of his ill-tempered, middle-aged teacher, Mrs. Bowers, "You know, Mother, I watched Mrs. Bowers in music lesson today (of course, she didn't know it), and I thought, 'You poor old thing, you're not really as bad as everyone says you are!'" - -

Would that everyone could be so forgiven for his wrongdoings!

* * *

Last week James put his arms around me and said, "Mom, I want you to know I really appreciate your teaching me to drive. I know it has been hard on you!" - - One of life's rewards - a word of appreciation from her child!

* * *

July 18

James's reason for giving $1.00 to the young man at Charlotte Square Shopping Center when he asked him to contribute to the "Dollarthon" for making a religious <u>film</u>: "I gave him the dollar because I thought he deserved it for putting himself in that embarrassing position of <u>asking</u> for it!"

Graham was really amused at James's reaction at having made the donation! He said, "James said, 'Damn Jesus freak!'"

* * *

Typical of the children's understanding of each other:

James said of Graham's new air rifle, "Don't take all of the <u>pleasure</u> out of it (to Mom and Dad) by giving him too many "do's and don'ts."

- 91 -

* * *

September 8

Graham, in one of his quizzically wise questions asked me yesterday afternoon when I picked him up at school, "Mom, do you know something I've found out? . . . Girls just RADIATE heat! . . . Why?"

* * *

October

Graham was riding along with me down Jocelyn Hollow, singing a song with words approximately like "With the shades pulled down, all day long with the shades pulled down. . . nobody knows what we're doing with the shades pulled down!". . .

I said, "Graham! Where did you hear that song?"

He said, "It's one you bought me on that Merle Haggard record!"

To which I replied, "Well, if I were you I wouldn't sing that where anyone could hear me."

"Why"

"Well, it's very suggestive."

"What's suggestive?"

"Well, it sounds as if something questionable is going on. . . like taking drugs or drinking, or something that shouldn't be going on."

Then, with a relieved, consoling, understanding look on his face, he smiled sweetly at me and said, "Oh, Mom, you don't have to worry. That's not what they're doing! They're just making LOVE!"

* * *

George's favorite incident of the summer Martha Sills had finally become absolutely "in love" with tennis. When work was over in the afternoon, she'd come home and immediately get dressed to go out for a lesson or a game before dinner. One afternoon she spent a goodly amount of time getting dressed just right, in just right, most fashionable name-brand tennis clothes. Then she said a brief goodbye and rushed breathlessly out the front door to her game. About two minutes later she came rushing in again. George yelled, "What's the matter?"

"Oh, I forgot my <u>tennis racket</u>!"

* * *

Martha worked in a health foods store in Franklin at Carter's Court the summer after her freshman year in college at Samford University. Her job was to make loaves of whole wheat bread. She was so pleased with the beautiful loaves she was making that she announced to me, "I know how I'm going to make some extra money next fall! I'm going to make loaves of bread and sell them in the dormitory on Saturday mornings!"

When the summer was over and she had finished her last day at work, she came home and announced like a just-released slave, "I don't _ever_ plan to make another loaf of bread as _long_ as I _live_!"

* * *

Graham . . . Grade Four
Danny may be smarter on the _outside_, but I'm smarter on the _inside_.

* * *

January 22

Last night Graham came to George and me and wanted to know what the meaning of the word "guardian" is. I explained to him that it showed legal ownership or responsibility of a grownup person for a minor, or a child. "When James's father died, for instance, I had to be appointed legal guardian for Martha, Elizabeth, and James because he did not leave a will."

In great excitement, Graham asked, "Then who got the _souvenirs_?"

Of course, I then explained to him that the court had to divide everything that was left in his name. . .

We were much amused at his use of the term "souvenirs."

This morning I told James what Graham had called the property his father had left. James said, "Well, I call those things "<u>inanimate</u> survivors.""

* * *

Two pleasant memories of Graham, aged eight. . .

When he kept having trouble with a shirt in finding out which was the front, which the back, he took a magic marker and wrote in bold letters on the front, "SIDE I"!

On being asked if he had ever seen a program or heard of Charlemagne he said, "No, but I've heard of chow mien!" . . . With which he laughed whole-heartedly!

He said he didn't mind being descended from a <u>king</u>, it was, after all better than being descended from a general like Nathan Bedford Forest, but he certainly didn't want to be kin to a <u>stupid</u> king like King John!

* * *

At the State CAR Board Meeting at Nero's Cactus Canyon when Graham was about eight or nine years old, he sat still and quiet as long as he possibly could. Then he blurted out when there was a lull in the business, "Now I know why they call this a <u>bored</u>

meeting!" The president, a teen-aged girl from Clarksville, gasped and pretended she was going to hit him as the other people, young and adult laughed.

* * *

NEW YEAR'S RESOLUTION
"To be able, at all times, to see thyself in my household kettle!"

Charlotte B. Perry

Neither shall I let the grass grow under my feet as this is the year in which my hourglass is to be turned upside down, even though I should live to be a hundred.

* * *

One most unforgettable memory of Graham, aged eight years, grade three:

Mrs. Gattis, the teacher, had reminded Graham <u>not</u> to <u>jump</u> off the stage when he finished his speech in the contest that afternoon. She was well aware of his vivacious, spirited, natural instinct to bounce and jump around.

He recited four poems he had written himself. The audience responded with appreciation and great amusement, and Graham, relieved and much pleased with himself, finished, smiled and then took one great big jump off the stage (one step high). In the middle of the jump he was suddenly quite aware of his mistake! He was almost instantaneously suspended in air, the bright smile frozen in a look of horror at his mistake. One could tell that the only remedy in the world would have been an "Instant Replay" camera running in reverse!

In talking with the teacher later I found that she, too, was just as amused as I was! At least once in her life she had seen a student who was genuinely <u>sorry</u> for having disobeyed her! That incredible look on his face was evidence of his remorse!

* * *

Graham:

Mrs. Venable, please don't tell Liz. But I'm sort of her slave. Don't tell her this. I know you like her, and I like her, too, but when she's home I'm sort of like her slave. It gets to my mind sometimes. You know how you told me noise wouldn't bother the raccoons! Well, one night I came out talking loud to feed them, and she said, 'Shut up, you'll make the raccoons run away.' I told her, 'Mrs. Venable said noise doesn't bother them,' and she said, 'Shut up. I want to hear the Olympics.' Sometimes it just gets to my mind."

About Nadia C. - "I guess we won't ever get married because we're from different countries (she's Rumanian), and she wouldn't understand the way I think."

* * *

Graham's assessment of his basketball coach, Steve Edwards: "He uses <u>reverse</u> psychology on us, Mother, and it backfires!"

* * *

A basketball game played at Linden, Tenn., was a real rout at 67 to 27. Graham had only three fouls in the last quarter, so at a time out he said, "Mr. Edwards, I am <u>expendable</u> for two more fouls. Is it all right if I go back in there and just <u>use</u> one of them?"

The coach grinned, so Graham tried to make one big, splashing foul on a man who was headed in for a layup. Instead of hitting the <u>man</u> with all his might, he hit the ball! Surprise! It was a real case of "I couldn't have done it if I'd tried!"

* * *

July 28

Graham rode his bike three miles down Jocelyn Hollow with one pedal broken. He telephoned and said, "Mom, don't worry, I rode my bike because it was downhill all the way!"

"But, Graham, what if you'd had to put on brakes?!"

"Oh, Mom, you're really <u>behind times</u>! The brake of a ten-speed is on the handles!"

* * *

George and Graham spent some time one night this week discussing the Perry family. They concluded that they were actually not only father and son, but because of intermarriage in the family four generations ago, they are actually fifth cousins. (I don't know how many "times removed.")

During the course of the conversation Graham asked George a question he couldn't answer. "That's all right," he said, "I'll ask Aunt Margaret. Women always know more about things like that than men."

* * *

Martha Sills stopped at the front door as she was leaving for Samford Tuesday morning. I told her I loved her very much and was proud of her, to which she replied that she "knew". At that time she made a little declaration of hope and confidence that any mother would have loved to hear from her 19-year-old daughter.

"I have made friends on my own, and I have worked hard this first semester to find a place for myself. I have accomplished a lot since I've been at Samford, and I am really [humbly said] proud of that."

Martha has not always been confident enough. When I think of the many times I've had to "hold her hand," so to speak, of how she would not go in a store by herself, or cross the street alone, I am really exceptionally happy that she is finding her measure of independence and is enjoying it. Martha has much to offer in this world. . . I am happy for the people who will get to know and love her.

The occasion of her being at home on <u>Tuesday</u> morning was a thing of amusement in itself. The Vanderbilt team was playing its final game against Alabama. She came home to see the "F Troop" play its last game. She was really a devoted and loyal fan to the end and conceded that there really is such a thing in basketball as "home cooking", only this time it was not Vandy who received it!

* * *

March 1978

Upon asking Graham just what he thought his soul was like, he responded: "Well, I've always thought it was in the shape of Sicily, and I thought when you died, your soul went up somewhere in the sky and it looked like Sicily."

* * *

December 2, 1978

This will indicate that I truly believe yesterday entered Graham into manhood! When he played a great game of soccer at Battle Ground Academy, a boy called him a "bitch," and he told him to "go to hell!"

He and Ben were up until the wee hours of the morning playing war games (Squad Leader), and at midnight they made themselves a pizza, the remains of which were on a plate this morning along with the remnants of a can of <u>sardines</u> that they had eaten.

Soccer! Cussing back! War games! Pizza! And sardines! At 13, I'd say that a few other realizations aren't far ahead!

* * *

When Graham was in his early teens, big brother James said, "Graham, it is time you stopped telling Mother everything! You're on your own now!"

* * *

Note for Graham's lunch bag when he attended the French Festival at Battle Ground - April, 1979 - 'Qu 'est-que c'est?

Il est un peu (pew!) nourriture! Mangee! S'il vous plait!

Le turquie! Suppose il est bon! Je n'ai pas tout autre!

Mere

He won 1st prize for name tag design.

* * *

March 12,

My 53rd birthday!

I called Mother to let her know that I was thinking about her. She had just gotten out of the hospital on Saturday, but this morning with the spring sun shining brightly, she had walked down to get the mail. On the way back she spied a clump of crocuses in bloom, but they were where she would not be able to see them when she went back in the house. She, therefore, got a spade and dug the whole clump up and replanted it where the old cedar tree had been so that she could look out the dining room window and enjoy them in blossom! Mother has the eternal eye for beauty and a nature that soars even from despair with the sight or sound of anything lovely. I do hope I can be the same way as I grow old.

* * *

March 29

Note from James after I had marinated a steak,
cooked it and asked him to get together his own dinner
while we went with Graham to his basketball banquet.

Dear Mom,

Why weren't you home to cook me dinner? The
steak was so dry because I didn't warm it up long
enough.

James

* * *

March 19, 1979

At the Harding Academy basketball banquet
tonight, Graham won two awards: "Hustler," which is
engraved and on display at school permanently <u>and</u>
"Most Valuable Player." (He wore his daddy's shoes
since his feet had out-grown his own! Symbolic?
Maybe.)

On receiving the "Hustle" award first, quite
unexpectedly, he made the little speech he had
thought up because he <u>thought</u> he was going to get the
"Most V.P." He said later, "Gosh, I didn't think I could
possibly get two, so I decided to say it <u>then</u>!"

Said Graham, "This award is not just for <u>me</u>. It's for <u>all</u> the team because they <u>all</u> deserve it!."

Shirley Harvey said, "He's the most adorable child I've ever seen. He greeted me at the door and said, 'Welcome Mrs. Harvey, I hope you have a good time!"

* * *

George - May 28 (Memorial Day), 1979

"It's no fun to have a holiday when you're <u>retired</u>!"

* * *

September 20

Diamond nor star could rival the sparkle of a raindrop pinnacled to a tall sprig of grass when the sun shines after a gentle morning September rain!

* * *

November 7

What a wonderfully meaningful time of life!

This morning (Sunday) I found an ashtray (in the den) filled with pipe ashes (Ben and Graham had been smoking their Black Forest pipes), and in the kitchen sink were two empty <u>hot chocolate</u> cups!

Ah, Boys!

God bless them as they grow into adulthood!

* * *

Graham said that at Hillwood High School when they say the "Pledge of Allegiance to the Flag of the

U.S.," a lot of people end it with "liberty and justice for some!" Otherwise they do not stand up or say it at all as in his co-op class - "not a single one stood."

* * *

November 7

Graham's observations on "College Board Exam" he took yesterday!!

"You know that test was just filled with questions and material about blacks and not a single black person was in the room taking the test!"

"You could tell that the test was prepared by minorities. They were all either women or Polish or Jews or blacks."

* * *

November 21

"I do hope if God ever decides to destroy the world, I do hope he'll leave England!"

Graham

* * *

November

When the coach called Saturday A.M. to find out why Graham wasn't at basketball (church) practice, he said, "I've been working hard every night this week on the 'Senior Varsity Show.' That's the most important thing to me these days because it's the first time I've ever had an opportunity to do anything for my school!"

* * *

As I "put out" the three Santa Claus shepherds Jean Gibson had given the children for Christmas 1961 (our first in Greensboro), I remembered how Martha Sills used to go by them, turn a bit and say coyly, "While the shepherds watched their <u>flops</u> by night!"

* * *

Christmas Day

Mother: "Elizabeth, I read that eating sweets and drinking alcohol can both cause depression (during the holidays).

Eliz: "Well, I'll tell you that sweets are <u>more</u> depressing than alcohol!"

* * *

After Christmas was over and everyone else had gone home, Graham said: "Mom, you know each one of us [children] has his own special, one-on-one relationship with you. I've just noticed it - that is instead of <u>all</u> of us having a relationship <u>together</u> with you."

I guess that is a result of my sincerely trying to make each individual child <u>special</u> in his own way.

Who knows if that were right or wrong? I just loved and respected each one for his <u>own</u> ways and personality.

* * *

January 21

Wonderful, sentimental day!

Warm inside, ice storm outside has weighted down the branches of the trees and every living thing, coating every holly and berry in a quarter of an inch of glistening splendor! My beloved cedar lies on the ground, its hulk like the grizzled icy beard of a North West lumberjack in sub-zero weather! It really makes me sad to see its helplessness, my delightful tree yielded to the elements!

Graham has spent the day <u>moving</u> from Martha's room, which he confiscated for himself three or four years ago when she left the nest and went to Dallas to live. How that much musical equipment, multitude of games, papers, etc., could have collected into one small spot is beyond my imagination! It had become a place simply <u>overrun</u>!

I suggested that he bring James's bed into Martha's room and take his belongings into James's room. It was a very practical and happy solution to a real living quarters problem. Graham spent the <u>whole</u> day moving, and at 10:30 p.m., although things are still in turmoil, there is an inkling that they can be straightened out.

- - But - - As I prepare to go to bed, I am suddenly SAD - sad with the realization that this move means I don't really ever expect dear James to need his room for his personal living quarters again. And the tears I am shedding are for the dear boy who once belonged in that room and needed it for his home. Oh! And then I remember the same pangs when Elizabeth and Martha left us and their rooms were "up for grabs" to take on other uses for the remaining family!

How dear it is to remember each separate child in his own separate room! Even though they were small rooms, crowded beyond imagination sometimes with personal belongings, how lucky we all were that they could have their own little sanctuaries! How I treasure the trips I made in to each to kiss my darlings goodnight! How bittersweet to remember them in their own personal settings!

How empty each room seems without its own child of the growing-up years! How possible it is in my imagination to place them there again!

I realize tonight more than ever that each one of

my children has a permanent room - a permanent home - and that it is in my <u>heart</u>!

I'm sad tonight that James's room has been transformed into Graham's room - but I'm going to be glad that Graham still has a few years to make it his own. The time will come too soon when he leaves the room, too, for a place of his own, and then I'll wander through a whole house with only memories of my dear children!

How I love them, each separate one! How wonderful I think they really are!

* * *

January 22

George dispelled in one brief statement the fears I had had about suddenly bringing upon him the responsibilities of "fatherhood" at age 48 when he became the father of four, practically at once!

This morning he said, "Do you realize how <u>lucky</u> we are still to be so close to children at <u>our</u> age! Just think, I'm 67, and we <u>still</u> have one at home!"

This was his response to me when I told him I'd cried last night about having James's room, as he knew it, taken over by Graham.

* * *

January 29

This week James reminded me that my children could learn science (chemistry, etc.). It's just that "they don't want to spend the time to learn it!"

I think my children inherited this from me. Instead of working to learn something, I think of myself as running barefooted through a field of blooming poppies. I thought of that when seeing a red field of them blowing in the breeze in County of Kent, England, this summer! In thinking of life this way, I guess I'm always expecting to see Dover Beach at the end of the way!

* * *

February 3

Today I think I've joined the ranks of the contemporary poets! My thoughts have become collages, the smooth ebb and flow of spring-like youth has gone, and there are too many things on my mind. Like a TV program designed to show, in 10 minutes, all of the baseball action of the past time prior to this World Series, including world events like Hitler's rise to power, the destruction of the Von Hindenburg over Lakeurst, and the Easter Parade of 1948. Thoughts come skipping and pushing and galloping through my consciousness.

Last night there was Zubin Mehta conducting Beethoven's Ninth Symphony with the contra bassoon still thumping, bum-bum, bum bum bum, ba boom, ba boom, bum bum! This morning there are traces of snow showing on the rooftops of houses heretofore hidden in the grey-brown of the surrounding hills. The precipitation is falling in icy sparseness, now and then, and we have walked four miles in Stephen Von Augs' "Appalachian Spring" weather. The quince bushes are in full color, if not wide-open blossom, with the honeysuckle bushes named "first breath of spring" by my mother showing their flowers and holding their jasmine-sweet essence for a warming-up during the day. Yesterday's wonderful lunch, De's cherry cobbler, the open fire and the Scrabble game with her wonderful new Our-Heritage Dictionary (How I love dictionaries!) and the commercially obscene Scrabble Dictionary on the card table come back to entertain me still.

The cardinals fly at the bird feeder, and a downy woodpecker climbs daintily up and down the peach tree's bitter branches looking for insects (I suppose). The clock goes tick, tick, tick, tick, in four-four time and beyond that the stillness of the house can be heard and felt.

But the ever-present collage keeps bringing back a memory from the early morning news, and I hear "Steven Aug reports the economic news. Steven Aug!" Upon that humorous note I will close! One can no longer get away from the influence of television, and all of the beauty, the quality, the meaning of contemporary life is hammered at in staccato from the "boob tube" as snowfalls and firelight, familial loves and times of creativity are constantly punctuated by "hard-sell," Madison Avenue TV! How lucky were Rousseau's children!

* * *

February 11

To show that my 81-year-old mother is "up with the times!"

On the phone a few minutes ago, we were discussing bluebirds. She had seen four or five of them several times in the little apple tree in front of her kitchen window.

Mother: "These were the little blue birds with brownish-red breasts and a bit of white."

Charlotte: "They were the 'Eastern Bluebirds'!"

Mother: "Well, the kind we used to think were <u>real</u> bluebirds were the little tiny ones that were blue all over!"

Charlotte: "You're talking about the blue <u>buntings</u>. We had them at one time, but we don't see them any more - only the larger ones now."

Mother: "Well, maybe they've <u>integrated</u> now!"

* * *

February 10

Graham was explaining about Mr. Durham's saying that he was "going to ride his little cart right into the space age and any 'liberals' who wanted to get on with him would be welcomed to a ride."

Graham said: "You know, Mother, I've decided what the difference is between "liberals" and "conservatives." The "liberals" want peace at any price - just so there's harmony <u>right now</u>; but the conservatives have a <u>goal in mind</u>, and they're willing to make mistakes along the way just as long as they have something <u>ahead</u> that they truly <u>believe</u> in!"

Boy! If that doesn't sum up the "liberals" <u>and</u> 'conservatives" I know!

* * *

April 16

All of a sudden I have seen the <u>humor</u> in growing older! I might as well!

This morning I started preparing dinner for guests for the first time in months. I remembered how many hundreds, "yea" thousands, of times I have done so before. Somehow I couldn't get into the "swing of things." I can no longer season food since George is on a strict diet, and I was suddenly faced with salting and peppering and buttering again!

The climax to my comedy of errors this morning, which really made me laugh - at myself - at circumstances - at the inevitability of things, went something like this:

What to have for dessert? Something <u>easy</u>, of course; something I would <u>not like</u> well enough to <u>finish</u> after the guests had gone; something I had the ingredients for - a chess pie! Certainly that would be easiest, best, most likely <u>all</u> eaten up at one sitting. Besides, Graham likes that! So - I made a batch of the "quick pie crust" and put it into the refrigerator to chill until firm.

Early Pear Blossoms

In the meantime, I started looking for a recipe for curried fruit, to go with the dinner. As usual, I lost myself in the fascination of "going through recipes." That has always been more scintillating than reading fairy tales to me!

Suddenly, I came across a recipe for Rum Cake. Gosh! That would be good for tonight's dessert. So I got out the lovely Bundt pan, floured and buttered it, got out all of the ingredients, including the bottle of rum I'd bought just for such an occasion.

I hated all of the butter on my hands, the excess flour that fell into the sink when I prepared the Bundt pan, but it actually wasn't <u>so</u> bad! I just felt a little awkward with my arthritic hands.

Then I got out the mixer, the eggs, the bowl, and went to the cabinet for the Jell-O Instant Pudding Mix. All went well except for the little hole <u>somewhere</u> in the Jell-O package that gently, steadily, sifted fine Jell-O powder from the shelf, down to the floor, into my open "slide" shoes, between my toes! A little wet paper towel remedied that, so on with the cake making!

I mixed the thickish batter, resisting the temptation to put in "just a little <u>more</u> rum!" Since my hands are now a (very) little awkward, I moved the floured pan to a small, low table in the middle of the room. Having a difficult time holding the mixing bowl and pouring at the same time, I sort of edged my way around the table and the pan at the same time. Then I stepped into the bowl of water we keep under the table for the dog! Damn! And my feet were wet. But I couldn't stop pouring cake batter at that stage! All of a sudden my half glasses began to slip and head for the batter in the bowl! I couldn't turn loose the bowl; I couldn't reach for my glasses, so I called George - poor, almost deaf George.

Then I screamed for George whose movements rival those of the celebrated tortoise who raced the hare! On second call - no, yell - he heard me - and arrived just in time to catch my falling glasses! I continued to pour the batter around in the Bundt pan!

Finis! All finished and I moved to the sink to put water in the sticky bowl and to wash my hands. Relief! Perseverance had triumphed!

I slipped the cake into the preheated oven and closed the door.

What to do next?

I opened the door of the refrigerator for the butter to go in the icing. What did I see immediately in front of my eyes? The freshly made piecrust, of course! In twenty minutes I had forgotten that I was going to serve chess pie for dessert and had <u>already made</u> the crust!

Oh well, the rum cake smells good cooking and I think I'll complete the chess pie anyway! Maybe we'll just have dessert tomorrow, too!

How funny! At least I realize that some of the best times in my life are the ones I've had laughing at myself!

Oops, I just remembered I forgot to see what time it was when I put the cake in the oven! I'll just guess at an hour! Thank heavens for a glass, see-through oven door! At least I'll know if it begins to burn!

Sequel to the foregoing:

Famous last words: "At least I'll know if it begins to burn!"

The phone rang, and I became engaged in conversation with Overton Ward. We talked about everything under the sun except cooking cakes. When I hung up <u>much</u> later, it was "by the grace of God" that I even thought of the cake again - and - it <u>did</u> burn but not so much that <u>I</u> can't eat it. Maybe it is too burned for the company! Ha!

* * *

Graham's third day at Battle Ground Academy

When Graham started to talk about "what went on at school today," I asked him if he ever saw Mr. Bragg (the headmaster).

He said, "Yeah."

I asked, "Does he ever speak to you?"

"Yes"

"What does he say?"

"Oh, he says 'Hi.'"

I asked, "Do you ever speak to him?"

"Yes."

"What do you say?"

"Oh, I just say 'Hi.'"

Later, Graham said that his English teacher was young, just out of college, but he believed she <u>knew</u> the subject and would be a good teacher.

A student who flunked Algebra last year and is in Graham's class this year said, "This teacher just spits out algebra, and he isn't teaching us anything." Graham said, "I think he's wrong. I think he is a good teacher, and I understand what he is saying. I'm going to keep up with the class, and I think I'm going to learn something."

"The speech teacher is just great. She asked us to name our pet peeves, three of them. I told her I only had one, and it is Tommy Andrews!" She also said that she just loved all of her students. A boy, labeled a "brain" got up in speech class and said, "There are three members of my family. They are <u>myself</u>, my mother and my father." Graham just laughed because a "brain had misused myself!"

"The science teacher is a little mean, but I'm not afraid of her. I guess it'll be all right."

"The French teacher is weird, you're right, but I think I'm going to be able to learn French better than last year because she said we weren't going to <u>memorize</u> a list of words. We're going to memorize them and really learn them by <u>using</u> them in our class. . . Last year we just memorized a list!"

"Now, Mom, I don't want you and Dad to think I'm going to be the <u>fastest</u> person on the basketball court."

"I didn't think you were going to be." I said. "Dad and I just want you to have a chance to play and to enjoy yourself."

"Well, I was afraid you thought I was going to be the fastest, and I didn't want you to be disappointed!"

(Today he came home and said, "It's going to be pretty good in basketball. That floor has springs to it, and I can really jump high!")

"Mom, you know the food at BGA isn't as bad as everyone says it is! I think they're all just saying all those awful things about it to have something to talk about. I think I'm going to be able to eat it."

As for having to ride the bus those forty miles a day he said, "I'm going to like riding the bus because the boys on it are different from the ones I have classes with. That way I'm going to meet a lot more people and have more friends!"

"One boy got up at the front of the bus the first day, beat himself on the chest, raised his arms and said, 'Battle Ground Academy! That's a great sounding name for a school! It's going to be great!' And you know, Mom, I think he's right!"

This is about as positive an attitude as I've ever had from a child at school. It will certainly be interesting to see whether or not it continues!

* * *

My Close Relative

My closest relative is my brother, James, a tall, dark haired sixteen-year-old man. Well, I guess I could consider him a man. He stands about five feet, eleven and a half inches tall and is the strongest guy I have ever seen. One thing that makes him strong is that he can lift over seventy pounds with one arm. Of course seventy is the most he has ever tried to lift that way. He is a good friend to go fishing with even though he catches all the fish. He is good at four sports. They include football, basketball, baseball and, most of all, hunting! He killed his first deer this year and is going for another. I can't wait for the day I can hunt with him. He makes high honors in school and is really my best friend.

December

* * *

I find that, although the <u>theorists'</u> theory is actually <u>valid</u> and <u>operating</u>, it would serve, <u>if</u> understood and <u>consciously</u> applied by <u>man</u> (common, ordinary, en mass man) to reduce him again to original form (state, energy, etc.)(much as man seems psychologically bent on self-destruction or death)-

(After reading "On Time and Space" by McLuhan)(can be applied to modern art, music, especially in its new recognition of dimensions)

C.B.P.

* * *

Graham

"Jehovah phobia" - fear of God

his own interpretation

* * *

August 6

Last night I dreamed a dream of Old Belford
Church. . .but it was not just a dream of a church.

My dream was a dream of something familiar and
dear, of something that has disappeared from the
scene in reality, but of something so real, so vital and
so indelible in the days of my childhood, it is ever with
me although it could no doubt only be summoned
from the world of dreams by whatever stimulus
(unknown and uninvited) could activate the channels
to bring it back. . . However the world of the un-
conscious works, last night it revisited for me the
scene of my Sunday mornings as a child, and of much
more. The aura of the weathered, old building itself
was there as I peered through a door that was a
creation of the dream, one that had actually not
existed. The new door through which I viewed the
remaining members of the congregation gathered for
the service was a creation through which I could leave
the actual, wide double doors with the white china

knobs untouched and therefore more real. Consequently, I was there! I felt the somber mood of the people who had been my friends. . . They sat silently, in blue serge and dark clothes, still and serious, filling the pews on the right-hand side of the aisle, which was dominated by the oblong iron stove browning with its patina of growing rust. Strange and appropriate thing, thirty years later as it is, everyone was older, much older. I alone seemed to be the same.

As the dream proceeded, people seemed to wander toward the old cemetery through which I had wandered so often as a little girl. I could still smell the pungent, yet tart odor of the aging arborvitae and feel the soft fragrant presence of the mimosa in bloom as the gentle breeze played with the waving slender branches. . . Yet I did not go with the people to visit the old graveyard and its crumbling, weathered stones which had so captivated me and my imagination as a child. . . I moved on toward the front, out of the gritty, hardened path of the circular drive, into the grassy, weedy hillside that separated the church from the road. I did not seem to be alone. There was a presence although I could not see her, and I think it was my sister, Martha.

I stooped down, gently, but as if compelled. And there it was, the loveliest of all my childhood memories. . . the dainty lavender-blue of a tiny clump of bluets, the Quaker Lady I loved. Before the weeds and grass of the summer ever had a chance to grow and overwhelm, the hill always seemed to be covered in a delicate carpet of bluets, their tender, fragile stems bending willingly in the breeze as if to captivate and call attention unless they go unnoticed because of their un-commanding size and lack of commanding hue and intensity. Here in my dream it was a perfect clump, with a leafy base seeming broader than I remembered, spreading itself to call attention to its presence. I touched the flowers, and the feeling was good. I remembered. I was there again. . . but there seemed all about a sadness. The sadness was not offensive or overwhelming, it was only there.

Then, as if the dream had a purpose, a point to bring home, we were back at my grandmother's old home. It was not the home built after the fire, or yet old Sylvilla, the original house at the edge of the wood. The house was the "big" house that I first actually knew. It was the house in which I was born, and we were at the door of the kitchen opened onto the long back porch. My father was there, my aunt was there,

and with us were several others. No one had to say it.
All of us knew that we were the ones remaining. All of
the good times, the love we had known, and the
differences we had had were there in the grey sadness
that hung around. Words were not necessary, and
there were none. We were parting. It was as it should
be, but we knew what it was like to be left. The aura
was of acceptance tempered with sadness, and no one
had the will to fight or could be separated from the
past and all that it encompassed. It was as it should
be. In my dream I did not weep, but remembering as I
raised my head from my pillow, I found the tears
trickling down my cheeks.

* * *

Christmas

A wonderful time in spite of the devastating
conditions at home (Daddy confined in Louisburg
Hospital, never to return home, most likely. . . Louise
still at Duke since September, never to come home
again until her final resting place beside Granny and
Grandpa at Cedar Rock. . . Mother at home with Aunt
Dell there sick. . . Mother having suffered a bad fall. . .
Roger just out of the hospital on Christmas Eve with
his second spinal operation. . . Danny desperately

trying to run from one hospital to another and to keep things together. . .)

In spite of worry hovering about like a storm cloud, it was a warm, loving, happy time here. Liz and Dave came to have Christmas dinner bringing the Yorkshire, Puddin, scampering in with a red Christmas bow on her neck and lots of presents for us all. . . Daddy's medals and war memorabilia attractively arranged on a pretty blue velvet background, an antique split tray to hold my silverware, etc.

Martha Sills was happy to be at home with us. She helped me with the dishes and cleaning the kitchen all during the holidays. What a difference it made in my load! Christmas morning before dinner she came in and announced to me that she had given herself the best present of all. . . namely that she had stuck with her college work and prepared to do what she really wanted to do! A great present for me, too!

At six a.m., I could no longer sleep, so I got up, awakened Graham, who said he had gone to sleep, aged 13, without the Christmas spirit for the first time in his life! He had a good day in spite of the new feeling of having outgrown the childish anticipation of Santa Claus. He practiced shooting basketball goals in anticipation of his first real year of playing basketball and being captain of the Harding Academy team. Several times during the day he reminded George and me of what wonderful parents he thought we were!

James spent a good part of the holiday season deer hunting. He would get up around three a.m., fix his own breakfast, and spend the rest of the day in the woods. He evidently loves being outside. The rest of the time he spent at his girlfriend's house, but he did seem to enjoy playing games with Graham a few times. He disappeared at mid-morning on Christmas Day, and when I found him he was in his room writing Christmas thank-you notes! Amazing sign of having grown up! The reward came when Alys Venable and Aunt Martha Burgess both declared they were going to keep their notes from James forever!

George and I had much love in our hearts for each other, our home and our wonderful children!

Love is where you find it, and happiness seems to follow the same pattern. On the one hand sadness, on the other joy! Christmas seems to be a time of concentrated amounts of both! With the spirit of Christmas as a catalyst for the mixture of the two, my hope is that the coming year will bring some periods of peace for all of us.

* * *

Today, September 8, is the kind of day that makes you realize that everything in life is worth the trouble!

The secret has to be the change of seasons! Would that I could remember the joy when the summer is hot and long, the winter cold and dreary! This September day has been so good, so full of the feelings that matter, I can hardly contain myself. It has held sensations of the joys of childhood, and it holds promise of the satisfactions of old age. Such a sweet September day is the elixir of life, and for the moment, I'm glad I have weathered the vicissitudes of fifty-five years just to know this sweetness.

I started the day with a four-mile walk with my friend, Charlotte Hancock, in the coolness of a misty rain so fine that it just seemed to exist around us like the cat-feet of Carl Sandburg's fog. Everything was green and alive as if ignoring the impending doom of fall and winter. The magnolia was green and waxed-like, filled with cones beginning to mature to red seedpods, but here and there high up in the tree there were a few white buds like the ones of May.

As the morning progressed, a hazy sunshine gradually penetrated the grey, and heavy dew disappeared from the grass and flowers. A few insects still buzzed as bee found blossom. At noon the temperature, according to the weather report, was 71 degrees. The sunshine, like the morning, just seemed to be, it seemed not intent upon demanding growth and opulence of the foliage. Its warmth was like an infusion of the most delicate, hovering nature, pleasant and lazy.

Goldenrod is barely turning yellow; wild Michaelmas daisies are in bud, but not bloom, though their cultivated counterparts are purple asters in bright, full splendor. Only the florets of the tall ironweed look more royal. In fact, there is one ironweed mass down the hollow so vividly purple and elegant that it would grace the solemnity of a cathedral or the bower of a king. Holly berries are bursting with green life, promising red for winter and cheer for the holidays. The polk berries are hanging ready for ripening in the weeks ahead, and the pear tree has already offered most of its abundant fruit to our taking. In its top still hang three or four of those voluptuous fruits, ripening each day for the moment that they release themselves for the drop to the ground with harshness that will bruise them and spill their juices for the late honey bees.

The afternoon sun is gradually sinking in the west. Shadows lengthen and the sunny areas of the grass brighten up the later afternoon with a yellow-green no artist could mix.

Day is almost over. Daddy has come home with the groceries. Life is good. Graham called to tell me that he is at Tommy's, and James has gone to get a haircut. Liz and Dave are vacationing at home, painting the kitchen and fixing up the house. Martha is teaching her little black-eyed Mexican children in Dallas.

What a wonderful family we are!

* * *

February 14

At the bird feeder:

a Carolina wren

titmouse

snowbird (ok, grey top, white breast)

hairy woodpecker

* * *

Charlotte Hancock and I signed up for a wildflower tour of Percy Warner Park.

The most heavenly experience of this bright, but nippy, spring morning was the creek that rushed straight toward the nature trail house, before making an abrupt right-angled turn in front of us. Such brilliance I have never seen in the largest diamonds! A near torrent of fresh water dashed against the stone and swirled forward, catching the sunlight in its very essence. A three-foot wide stream gushed and poured and pummeled and sprayed in the sunshine giving off sparkles of red and blue and yellow and orange and violet that cut into one's vision, imprinted itself on the mind, and brought forth gasps of sheer delight from the pit of one's stomach! As that wildly playful creek hit the bank in front of us, it turned to the right, slowed its pace and ran gracefully along a flat route toward the fields along the edge of the hillside.

We all piled into Metro-park trucks and headed into the park itself, through the trees making bowers overhead, and up the mountain. At the top we disembarked, having stopped briefly to listen to the sound of the birds, and our guide took us wending down the hillside to see the trillium and wild larkspur and violets of several varieties. An elderly gentleman guide pointed out the saxifrage which grew along the road bed, and told me it would grow in my rock wall. It was lovely, but it was not anything like the wonderful little flowers that grew in English walls at Cambridge. I am still looking for something like that to become the "flower in the crannied wall" as pointed out by the British romantics.

On our first descent, we saw a bluebird, its red breast shining and its blue so pure. Who knew bluebirds lived in a forest with trees towering hundreds of feet overhead? How tiny he looked up there; how gargantuan the trees; how free and untouchable that little bird!

Then we began our serious trek down the hill (mountain). There was barely a sign of a trail. The flowers grew into paths made the week before as if they had only been stymied momentarily. At points we had to climb over large dead logs three or four feet in diameter. Sometimes we made a trail of our own, each one exclaiming about his individual find. We saw phacelia, Canadian water plant, in full bloom. There were a couple of early Jack-in-the-pulpits, and different varieties of violets were everywhere. The most spectacular sighting was a hillside, perhaps a quarter of an acre, where yellow trout lilies, sometimes known as dog-toothed violets, bloomed all over the expanse. They hung their beautiful golden heads in the most graceful bit of modesty one could imagine, and their magic bells looked like flower hats painted by Wyeth in a scene of fairies at play in the woodlands of story.

At one point we met the bridle trail, and it gave us a much wider path toward the bottom of the mountain. Along it we found so many things growing. And as we looked back toward the left, by a huge old fallen tree, we spotted the white tail of a bunny rabbit, which was scampering at the sight and noise of our entourage.

As we left the trail to go past some brush, to see a very special flower, a snake moved in the bushes, and suddenly an excited young man began to ask, "What is this? What is this?" There was the most unusual, mushroom-looking lily of a thing. Its color was of black mixed with dust; its shape was of a four or five inch cupped-leaf bell. When the guide answered his call, she said excitedly, "Oh, that's Devil's urn." With that, she touched the point of her stick to its sides very gently and clouds of gray-black smoke rose from it. A memorable moment of the day, as she touched it again and again, evoking the same reaction from the mushroom.

The trucks picked us up at the Deep Well picnic area, and a tired lot of weary pilgrims climbed in to ride back to the park cabin.

Charlotte and I took off for the new Tennessee Barbecue place on Harding Road and enjoyed real smoke-cured pork served on corn cakes, a very hot sauce being our choice. Coupled with a few cups of very black, hot coffee, we satiated ourselves and gloated with the joy of a second wildflower trip through Percy Warner Park. We had seen ferns and water plantain, three kinds of trillium, dicots in the forms of nettle, purselane (spring beauty-claytonia virginica), white campion, and buttercup . . . common buttercup . . . larkspur. . . columbine and golden seal, laurel (spice bush), black-root, dutchman's breeches, bittercress and cut-toothwort, Shepard's purse, turning mustard, penny cress and Nashville mustard (all from the Cruciferae-mustard family), saxifrage, cinquefoil, wood-sorrel (oxalis)), geranium in the form of Carolina carnesbill, violets, do bane, blue phlox, all kinds of waterleaf from purple phacelia to baby blue eyes (which the guide had lifted ever so gently with her fingers), wild comfrey, mint in the forms of ground ivy and red dead nettle and henbit, plantain, bedstraw (both fragrant bedstraw and cleavers), all kinds of composite from dandelions and fleabanes to white bear's foot).

This is a real incentive to look forward to the flowering and leafing of each little plant in these wonderful Tennessee hills.

* * *

Purple

To me, the purple family seems, more than any other, to depend upon hue and intensity for its acceptance and palatability. Hence, the purple tulip tree in its final opening has "wormed" its way into my good graces, and all of a sudden, I think it's beautiful!

* * *

October 21

FREEDOM. . . can come too suddenly and with too much magnitude; then, like the over-sized leaf of a cottonwood tree on the breeze of a cool, bright September morning, it can be caught in the surge of the wind and turn rapidly graceful summersaults and precarious cartwheels hither and yon until the swelling wave of air slackens and dies. The leaf falls helplessly to the ground, powerless and finished, to be trodden underfoot by the passersby and rot with inactivity, the penalty of complete separation from the tree that produced its tender bud and nourishment for maturity.

FREEDOM. . . can be like the slowly emerging independence of a much-loved toddler who expresses his incorrigible zest for life in a hesitant step and finds that he can maintain his balance even beyond the reach of his parents' grasp. Another step or two produces even more satisfaction and growing confidence; but he alternates his forward progression with a backward look to his progenitor for the reassurance that fosters security and approval of a task accomplished. . . A wise parent does not beckon him to return, but in love and wisdom encourages the freedom being sought by his maturing offspring and hopes with the fervency of a prayer that he will be able to avoid the stumbling blocks that lie in his path, to emerge some day strong, able and full of understanding of the wiles that have tried to entice him from his forward course.

James heads for college Monday. I pray that the struggles of growing up will be assimilated with the love and support we have tried to give him, and that he will be able to tackle the new stage of development with the confidence of one to whom God has granted a large measure of ability and a family who loves him beyond measure.

* * *

October 28, 1979

"I couldn't begin to say how wonderful it was when I was at home with Mother and Daddy last week to have fresh butterbeans and homegrown corn, turnip salad from the backdoor garden, okra, tomatoes (those delicious firm, last of the season ones), sweet potatoes (first of the season, right-from-the-plowed-earth-ones), persimmon pudding, field peas (which I shelled while sitting in the front porch swing), fresh, tender crook-necked squash, plum jam, figs plucked from the bush, golden-speckled-amber scuppernongs from the vine, etc., etc.!" It all reads like a Southern novel. . . and the people were all just as friendly, kind and wonderful as they ought to be. . . unassuming, genuine and gracious to each other. Nowhere in the world are there such wonderful people as in Franklin and Nash Counties! I'm really glad it was my privilege to have been brought up there, and with Mother and Daddy for parents. Old age has changed their physical being and their mien, but deep down inside, they are still the most thoughtful, wonderful people in the world, and nothing can compare with the feeling that they are proud of me and that I can still make them happy, even if only for a brief few moments.

* * *

December 6

Today I have told Graham that it takes a much stronger man to sit on the bench than it does to get out on the basketball court and play a good game, especially when one <u>knows</u> that he could do just as well if he were given the same opportunity. I mean that with all my heart!

May Graham never have as little understanding as his coach does, and may he use his experience in freshman basketball at Battle Ground Academy under his coach to provide a basis for working with boys who are fighting the battle of growing up, proving their worth and becoming good men!

Battle Ground Academy, for the most part, has not provided the kind of instruction in athletics or academics that I have felt my boys needed. Exceptions to this are: Mrs. Lea, Mr. Herrman, Mr. McElroy, and James's geometry teacher. Graham's teachers still have to prove themselves at this writing. I do hope they will come through. I believe that every coach and every teacher should dedicate himself to bringing out the <u>best</u> in <u>every</u> child. Battle Ground Academy, as it seems today, serves best to establish an <u>elite group</u> made up of persons whom the personnel knows best from association with parents, etc.

* * *

Aged 14 - Graham's girlfriend asked him what he wanted her to give him for Christmas.

He smiled wickedly as he told me his reply, "<u>Money</u>!"

* * *

December 6

Mother called this morning. There is no one in the world as anxious to share happy thoughts and good cheer with others. Today she wanted to hope I was having a good 'rainy" day because she remembered that rainy days are my favorites.

Jeff Stokes had just paid them a visit. He had come to look for a cedar tree to make into a Christmas tree for his grandchildren who are coming to spend the holidays with him and Mary. Mother was touched, as am I, at the thought of an old man driving twenty miles to "the old place" to roam the land looking for a Christmas tree, on a wet, dreary morning. He showed up, drenched with rain-soaked old hunting clothes, paid them a visit, and then went out again to look for an appropriate cedar. I wish I had been there to point out the lovely new growth of cedars on the site of the old Belford Churchyard. I roamed among them this summer, reminiscing and longing to be able to cut one of the trees for Christmas myself! I'm glad someone else as sentimental as Jeff could do that!

Always looking for the humor and the excitement of any happening, Mother told of glancing out the window down toward "The House" yesterday morning just in time to see the old house turning slowly from back to front as if being carried on a giant "lazy Susan." Her response was one of absolute amazement and an absolute pinnacle of interest at the spectacle, which would have torn the heart out of me if I could have seen it! She could not know what a traumatic thing it is for me to realize that the house which was the center of my familial love for 45 years was being removed from its moorings and foundation, leaving in its wake a clear view of the farm and a monumental absence which will hang there in my memory as long as I live! Had her joy and excitement not been so innocent and so keyed with mirth, I would have gasped and wept. As she went along describing the scene, telling of its passing as it was being taken to its new home "not far away, over near Robert Marshall's house," I found myself caught up in the realization that one of life's most important facets is that each man can look at things from his own particular angle and arrive at a different conclusion. It is through that reality that one man can help another through a crisis and help to maintain a balance in this world, which makes living both bearable and good. Without realizing it (as I would never have told her) Mother had helped me to face a traumatic event, and within the scope of a few seconds, adjust to it with a good feeling - where Sylvilla once stood, with large hickory trees and giant oaks abounding its acres, grapevines, barns and the lot behind it. Mother said it looks lovely to gaze over the spot this morning, a tall pine and two large cedars only breaking the expanse. I still see the house, but I can imagine the tranquility that marks its place!

* * *

March 1

Today I know that my life together with George is slowly ending like the snowfall that is dwindling outside to a million minute flakes so small and light and uncertain that they are hardly perceptible. This morning the flakes were large and bold and beautiful. They came and left a heavy blanket of pure, blessed white, transforming the world everywhere they chose to fall.

Life with George has been much the same. Everywhere in my life that his steady, trustworthy, loving and helpful existence has touched me (and the children) there has been a beautiful, protective covering, which served as a buffer to all hurt, a balm for all feelings and a catalyst for all joys. The prospects of having him always have become a waning snowstorm which will no doubt end in nightfall. And the prospects of life without George are indeed as dark as night. My only hope is that the joys of life because of him will be so all-encompassing and widespread they will appear to me in the morning, after the dark, like the glittering blanket of snow, which, in the next day's sunlight lies bold and beautiful and pure in the morning sun.

* * *

July 1

Dear Graham:

If all has gone according to schedule, you have just taken off from Heathrow Airport in London on your way back to New York and the good old United States of America after fifteen days of your first European trip! How exciting to think about! Daddy and I have tried to visualize the time of day, what you'll be able to see that far north in the fading summer's light. I had hoped you'd be able to fly over Greenland and at least see it. Martha did, but Daddy says it's too far out, you'll be losing time. I accept his word. All I know is that soon you'll be home, and I've been considering what you'll be coming home to.

You'll be landing at that giant airport, Kennedy, on Long Island. The Holiday Inn will be your home tonight, and I'll bet there is between now and tomorrow noon when you leave N.Y. for Nashville a hamburger in the offing for a least one meal! Will you have time, or will you think, to take one cab ride into Manhattan since you've never been? Would it still dazzle your eyes and boggle your mind the way it does mine after you've seen London and Paris and Rome! I wonder!

Soon you'll be flying over the mountains and fields and lakes and rivers of Pennsylvania, West Virginia, Kentucky and Tennessee. Will any one of those still merit the distinction of "greenest state in the land of the free"? My uneducated guess is that you'll find Middle Tennessee so verdant and rolling and beautiful you will know the real meaning of "home." I can hardly wait to listen to you and observe and know how you feel to be back! A fifteen-year-old boy returning from his first trip abroad! My, my! How wonderful!

Should tomorrow be like today, our anxious, happy faces will greet you at the Metro Airport, and we'll bring you directly home to this lovely hill. The sun will be shining, and it will be getting progressively warmer and warmer, the kind of summertime that usually always precedes the Fourth of July. The bumblebees are now busy buzzing the hollyhocks and balsam blossoms. The summer breezes are moving the leaves of flower, tree and shrub, but they are warm. It is only after extreme exertion that one can sit still and feel the caress of those breezes and know the coolness of their touch. Perhaps they will blow up a few clouds, and we'll have another summer thunderstorm. It would, no doubt, bring welcomed rain as the grass and every living thing seems to have devoured the last showers with great desire. This early morning even brought out a baby rabbit to feed on the tender grass which a week before looked parched, brown and nearly dead. Everything looks so green! How many shades of that chlorophyll color show up in the various degrees of sunlight and shadow! Could the Maker have chosen any other color as wonderful as green to tie together the ends of the earth?

The Queen Anne's lace is still blooming airily like tiny snowflakes spread into three-inch circles. They bounce lazily on the slender green stems and an occasional butterfly lights on one momentarily as if

merely to display his beautiful wings. Up the grey
stone wall climbs the tenacious greenery of the
passion plant with its tendrils catching hold of
anything that gets in its path. Its blossoms boldly
stand out from the masses here and there, reminding
me of ballerinas in costume of daintiest lavender. The
herbs are blooming, even the oregano. The blue
flowers of the hyssop seem most aspiring, and the
purple marjoram even has little purple flowers where
stem meets leaf. The sweet peas have had their day of
pink bounty, and now they are filled with tender green
peas jauntily and prolifically adorning the vines. I
hope the green rose bushes are gathering their
"whatever it takes" to bloom again. I can still look at
them and remember how beautiful they looked a week
ago.

Daddy has spread grain on the wall as usual. The
course of the day brings out shapely grey doves, a
young flock (6) of blue jays, male and female cardinals,
a cowbird or two, and at least four squirrels. The
chipmunk appears in the terra cotta drainpipe hole,
peers warily out, and suddenly scampers the length of
the wall to get his fill of the free seeds spread out

Snow and the Sunlight off Daffodils

there. A strange little noise on the back porch can, a few minutes later, bespeak the fact that this roguish little devil is now inside the bag of seeds, greedily filling his pouches. How differently he goes about feeding himself from the elegant, sleek dove which pecks here and there occasionally, seeming to select one seed in preference to another!

All out of doors will be waiting for you, son, but the cradle of your welcome will be inside your home. How clean it has been for two weeks! How organized and straight! But your busy, enterprising self has been much in absentia! I don't believe you've ever given me a feeling that you've been bored. You are constantly at work entertaining yourself or a friend. You build; you play a musical instrument; you draw; you sing; you play games. Always you seem to be going in and out, playing basketball, riding your bike or taking to the phone to talk personably to a friend. I see you reading, mostly materials for the complicated games that you and Ben play, or maps. I hear the typewriter going and know that you are recording some voluminous list of information connected with your entertainment. A burst of song or a loud roll of music from the organ is never unexpected or unwelcome!

And not to forget the guitar! I might even say I've missed that!

Home again will mean the beginning of activity to which you have been accustomed. It will mean sleeping in your own bed, Martha's bed, that is! Somehow you never seem to get the "things" of your own; you have confiscated your sister's bed and room and the quiet sanctity that it affords from the rest of us. That feminine spot will soon sport piles of damp, wet beach towels, rings of trousers left on its floor! There will be a wastebasket filled to overflowing with balls of used paper, and the little antique table will be laden with empty, used glasses and candy wrappers.

The dirty clothesbasket will fill up and push the doors ajar in the hall. The back of your bathroom sink will have an odd assortment of bottles, tubes, and indiscernible things, including drying squirts of things like toothpaste and shampoo.

In short, you will be home, and all will resume its natural course for a fifteen-year-old boy. At least that is what we're looking forward to, and we hope you are looking forward to same.

How will your perspective be changed? I can't guess, and at this time, I guess it would be hard for

Blossoms and Greenery on the Back Wall

you to fathom it for yourself. I'm glad you could go! What an opportunity! I hope you'll be glad you did, but most of all, I hope you'll be glad to return. I hope the experience will be like a seasoning for your daily food. How it will have whetted your appetite, only time will tell!

Love,
Mother

* * *

We met Graham around noon at the airport. He was smiling, confident and happy. Daddy was driving and I sat in the back seat. Graham sat in the front seat with Dad, his left arm on the back of the seat, his head half-turned toward his father and to me.

"Well, I suppose you want to hear about my trip", he said.

From the back seat, "We surely do!"

"Well, when I got to England, I felt at home!" (Dramatic pause) "When I got to Paris - I <u>didn't</u> feel at home!" (He was with his BGA teacher and her French class.) "When I got to Switzerland - well, Mother, that's the most beautiful place I've ever been in my life and one day I'm going to take you there!"

He said nothing at all about Florence, which was next on the itinerary, but with great enthusiasm continued, "When I got to Rome - well, that's the most wonderful place in the world! I spent three whole hours in the Forum right by myself! And, Mother, I brought you something!"

Not really thinking things through, he had unearthed shards of pottery, tiny pieces from his wandering and had brought them to his mother. I was horrified but at the same time much honored that he wanted to share that wonderful walk in the Forum with me! The guide said, "Of course, you should not have taken these bits and pieces, but put them in a plastic bag on top of your clothing in your suitcase. They will take them out most likely when your bag is checked." But - they didn't and I cherished those shards for their historical value and the sentiment of a son's appreciation of his mother's love of history.

There were many wonderful stories to be told. I asked Graham if he liked Florence or learned much about Medicis. He said, "Well, I found a little bar with a <u>great</u> piano player in Florence, so I just sat and listened to his music and talked to him. I invited him to come to Nashville where the music really is!"

He didn't see David or any other beauties of Florence. To Graham, Florence was music. The world seems music to Graham!

He spent his last free hour in London in Hyde Park, and he gave his last English pounds to a man there who looked needy to Graham. They had also talked. Every man needs to be heard. Hyde Park is such a place for speaking and for listening. Graham does his share of both.

The highlight of the return to London was the trip Graham and Ben made to the World War II Museum on the other side of the Thames. What a twosome: Graham and Ben!

* * *

September 20

The drought was broken by raindrops falling gently from a sparsely clouded sky. One could tell that they were only a token promise that eventually there would be rain again - enough to quench the thirst of the trees and grass that had been tenacious enough to hold onto life. For the browned and parched vegetation unable to make the grade there was the caress of moisture and the sighing of the rains moving in like the sound of funeral music, a token of consolation mixed with promise for the future.

* * *

"Be with our children wherever they are. May we all have love in our hearts. Keep us safe."

Daddy (George Perry)
New Year's Eve, 1981
* * *

March 14, 1982

"We have <u>liberated</u> the human race into their own bondage."

C. Perry
Commentary on the times.
* * *

December 24

CEDAR reminds me of the things I remember about Christmas and the things I believe in about the preparations for celebrating the holiday. This morning I am clipping the leftover branches in preparation for making the wreath for our front door. The unequaled green-pungency of its odor brings clearly back the scenes of my childhood and the people I loved who played their part in my happiness: Granny Boone, Louise, Daddy, Mother, Martha and Danny, Granpa,

Aunt Marguerite, Uncle Richmond, Gray, Beverla, Uncle, and their children. Cedar trees <u>were</u> our Christmas trees, and this is the first time I have had a cedar tree in many years. The recession and the $25.00 trees at the tree headquarters ran us to the local pickup truck and the fresh native cedar trees for half that amount. As my mother would say, "All things work together for good. . ." Now cutting the leftover branches is a double reward.

My mood is not its best this year. Maybe it is my age; maybe it is "the Age." I seem to have lost my grip on an acceptable perspective. I do not understand people . . . friends, children, husbands, congressmen, presidents, not even myself. I long for respect and appreciation of my children, my friends, my husband. I do not see that I have had any good influence in the things which are important on the surface. I do feel that they are basically good and kind people and if they can come to terms with themselves I know that someday they will make their particular contributions to mankind. I have faith in them as persons; I guess I'm just weary of being their whipping post. I love to look at beautiful things; I've always tried to look and be neat, clean and attractive. I would so enjoy living in a reasonably orderly household. None of this seems important to most of the family. Martha seems to be the exception. Tonight she is coming home for Christmas, the first visit in a year. I hope to get the house in some kind of order to welcome her and to have something under the tree that will please her. She is thoughtful of others and does something about it. The others are thoughtful and caring, but they haven't learned to make the effort involved in letting others know. Discipline of self is the missing ingredient. My ability to keep up with "waiting on" the family has run down. I can no longer pick up enough wet towels, old envelopes, shoes, clothes, papers, cereal bowls, coffee cups, etc., to have any strength or time left to get the house to show off the beautiful things we have inside it.

This morning I am working on an attitude that will carry me through the holidays and make me a blessing to the children and George instead of a curse. I'm 57 years old, and today I'm fighting a battle with myself. I long for the simple, open-heart policy of unadulterated love and kindness and consideration in which I believe. Perhaps Danny's phone call has opened that door for me. She was baking last-minute things to take to Mother's, and she was in the Christmas spirit. I said, "James is the sweetest person; how I wish I could bear to look at him with all that awful hair and the beard!" She said, "Be glad he's there with you and overlook all of that!" How humble that made me feel. She has not seen Nicky for at least five years at Christmas, many times not even hearing from him. She loves him no less because of his frailties and mistakes, and she goes ahead laughing and working to make things happy for other people. Her tears are for her "closet." Her helpful, winning ways and person-ality are for everyone who comes in contact with her. I truly loved having her call me this morning to share her spirit with me, because I know deep down inside that she knows how I feel about things and that I am her kindred spirit.

Maybe I can now get back to work, a humble and forgiving and loving person, showing something of my best nature to the ones I love the most in the world. . . George, Elizabeth, Martha Sills, James, and Graham!

* * *

nuthatch

chickadee

goldfinch

towhee

cardinal

blue jay

Celebrating the Holiday

sparrow

squirrel

downy woodpecker

mockingbird

red-bellied woodpeckers

doves

starling

February 13 - the birds at our feeder today!

* * *

February 14

On the stone wall sunning himself sedately is a beautiful flicker. The sunshine glows on the yellowish feathers of his sloping back and tail. The red "V" at the back of his head is cadmium red deep and perfectly shaped, while the black "V" at his front throat is barely visible. He subtly and quietly turns his head once in a while but he is very placid and stationary and is certainly soaking up the spring-like sunshine.

His occasional looking toward the woods lets me know that, even in repose, this beautiful bird was alert to any approach of danger.

And surely enough - Stonewall, the brown and white spotted pointer (hound) appeared in the back yard and with a whirring flutter of gold, the flicker took off, exposing all of himself and his finery at once while exhibiting what the greys on nature's palate can do to enhance the most colorful of exhibits!

* * *

May 14

At no time of year is shadow more enhancing to sunlight and greenery than in May!

Outside the tenderness of the foliage is bouncing tauntingly in the breeze. The warm sunshine is wisely coaxing the young leaves to grow and mature, and the hillside is dazzled in waves of darkness and light as they (leaves) once again play in the gently stirring air. Here and there at

irregular intervals the long blooms of the hickory drop silently to the ground. Reddish-brown insects can be seen battling the springtime elements and the thrush has happened cautiously near our doorstep in search of food.

Last week, two of her developing brood crashed heedlessly into our large glass windows in the bright late afternoon sun and plummeted with broken necks to their death. Thus, on successive afternoons I wept at the waste of two songbirds that did not live to brighten our woods with the shrill beauty of their singing. Today, their parent is still here in quest of life, and perhaps she will produce another family.

I do hope there is a survivor of this spring's nesting somewhere around.

Clover is blooming cumulously in the grass, and the yellow iris is protruding boldly from its painted, green spikes. The daylily foliage is curving gently in masses above the stone wall. Bits of color dot the flower buds in forms of lavender, purple, red, pink and white. My beloved lilacs have gone, but they, relics from my great grandmother's 19th Century garden at home, bloomed for the first time this year. I did not cut one of them for the house, but I daily pulled the blossoms gently toward me from their height so that I could enjoy their fragrance.

Now the sunshine comes and goes. I cannot see, but I can feel the presence of those billows of clouds passing high overhead. Perhaps we shall have rain later in the day. If so, more sustenance for all of this verdure!

May is my very favorite month! To think I only discovered it was so a few years ago. Now I treasure May like the welcomed, but infrequent visit of a dear friend.

I am even thrilled to know that I have sprung from an English family fortunate enough to have been named Mildmay! Mildmay of Cambridge. !

January 18

A four-inch snowfall during the night left us
blanketed in the most cozy warm and gratifying
circumstances today. It was as if the "Hand of the
Lord" had extended itself soothingly toward his weary
flock, enticed them to forget the ways of the world, and
to relish the peace and tranquility that only comes to
man when he separates himself from the contemporary rat race.

Nothing tangible is as pleasant as a pot of beans
(with ham hock) simmering the hours away on a
snowy day. The joy is in the lifting of the lid, the
stirring of the pot, the inhaling of the singular aroma:
beans, carrots, celery and old North Carolina ham.
Patience is of the essence. One knows from the
beginning that one cannot buy this kind of cooking.
Water boils away, must be replenished often in order
not to burn the treasure. The hard shells and
consistency of the beans are reluctant to give way to
the softening process. The palate is so primed with
excitement and flowing gastric juices ere long that
even the cook can hardly wait the meal and, during
the last hour, is constantly tasting the hot broth with
little staccato sips to see if the beans are done. Such

Stonewall

an experience was mine - and the results were no less than "super."

* * *

At 8:00 p.m., George and I watched a Smithsonian T.V. program, the subject "time." Marvelous revelations from years of study! The summation: "Time and light are one."

Afterwards, I walked from window to window looking out at the unbelievable beauty of a snowy moonlit night in these hills. Near midnight, I could no longer contain my urge to go outside and <u>experience</u> the night; to visually see the night was not enough.

I put on my fur hat and James's old down coat and stepped out into the cold. The weather forecaster had said it would be around 18°. Clear, clean air did not hit me in the face, did not shock my sensibilities. I simply opened the door, walked out into the glittering night, and the chill <u>was</u> all around me. I stood there in the cold and light and shadow that must have been the same as before the creation of the world. Gazing at the stars, I remembered the scientists' words: "Looking at the stars is looking <u>back</u> in time. The millions of years it takes for their light to appear to us assures that truth." I was looking up to the heavens.

I saw sharply twinkling stars; and I was looking <u>back</u> in time!

The nearness of the full moon has never been more apparent, and yet I knew how far away it was, thanks to our astronauts. Tonight, after looking at the distant stars, the moon seemed as near and familiar as a member of my own family. I remembered, while I gazed at it, how James, aged 4 years, had announced to George and me on a moonlit night: "I can <u>see</u> the man in the moon. I think he's just wiggled his ears." -- There was also Graham's excitement once when, as a little boy, he said: "I'll <u>swear</u>; I think I can see the <u>other</u> side of the moon!"

Wow! If I could only describe the out of doors tonight; the brightness of the moon the splintery light of the glittering stars; the shrouding, still cold; the perception of blue in the sky; grey clouds rolling here and there; penciled trees edged in white powdery snow; lights from homes nestled in the hills; white carpet of snow everywhere; no sounds anywhere, but I seemed to be hearing clearly with ears at the ready! As I gazed upward, I was aware of the most minute specks of brilliance! Hardly visible in the usual sense of seeing, I realized that the very moisture in the frozen air was reflecting and refracting the light!

I stood there in the snowy moonlight on the hillside we call "home," and as I gazed backward in time toward the stars, it came to be a part of me, that business of knowing that "Time and light are one."

* * *

May 20, 1983

Poor, dear Graham has just gone out into the dark gloomy, foreboding morning to attend the practice for his graduation ceremonies.

He was wearing an old green soccer shirt, some ragged "cut off" jeans, and in his hand he carried an Australian - stick. Around his neck he wore a string of tiger teeth.

"Oh, son, are you going to wear those?"

"Why not?"

"They'll think you're strange, and that's the way they'll remember you!" I said with a sinking feeling reminding me of the rejection he had received from the fellow students (and some teachers) in his high school years!

"At <u>least</u> they will <u>remember</u> me!" he said acidly as he hurried out the front door, which he closed with a sound slam.

* * *

Graham, as I perceive him:

"He was born with too tender, too loving a heart; but his over-expansive sensibility had attracted the mockery of his comrades."

Prosper Mérimée

as quoted in <u>Bryon</u> by André Maurois

* * *

August 12

Last night the 27-day drought was broken, and what a lovely occasion it was! All day long on news reports there were indications that a front was moving in from western Kentucky; but all day long the sun burned down and the temperature was a breathless 99 degrees. The air conditioning in my new car was on the blink; par for the course!

About twenty minutes to seven, the dinner already finished, lightening began to flash, the trees to bend down with the incoming winds, the thunder to boom, and suddenly there was rain! Even in the semi-darkness, the brown grass began to take on a hint of green. Within ten minutes we must have had an inch of rain. Within one split second following a terrific blast of thunder and a mighty streak of lightening, the lights were out. For the next three hours we were without current, and so the evening progressed.

Graham and three friends had gathered in the living room for a game of poker. With a variety of candles burning on my two nineteenth century candle stands, they noisily and good-humoredly played their games. George and I, feeling the stuffiness of the house, retired to the back porch to enjoy the freshness of the rain as soon as the storm subsided. There in the twilight, an eerie sort of yellow light surrounded the dense woods and hills from the outside, beyond them the sunlight still shone in the far west. We began to talk.

George was reminded by the boys' candlelight poker game of the days in North Africa in 1943 when he and other army officers played cards in the big square supply tent, far into the night. They made a poker table by covering two typewriter tables with blankets, and their light was, of course, the candles. From this memory he proceeded to talk about his days in the army, at my questioning and interest.

Musing that he had slept primarily on the ground for 2-1/2 years through North Africa, from Casablanca all the way to Tunis (Bizerte), from Tunis through the Invasion of Sicily, back to the barracks in England for a while, and then through France, Belgium and into

Germany. They (2nd Armored Division) were the first Americans into Berlin.

* * *

End of the Drought - September 3

During the hot, dry summer and the drought, which extended from June until September, the sun often shone hotly through a grey haze that blanketed the whole sky and seemed like a plague. Today, around noon, the invading darkness we perceived came from rolling clouds instead of the inexplicable smoothness of the previous weeks, and I felt that rain was in the offing.

With a few far-off rolls of thunder, the rains crept in and soon were falling in some kind of steady, gentle downpour. At first the wilted, thirsty dogwood leaves seemed to react to the moisture like a shy child overwhelmed by too much attention from visiting relatives. After ten minutes of refreshment, they seemed to have become acclimated to the thirst-quenching shower and were accepting, if not downright joyful, at their newfound pleasure. In half an hour, even the parched grass seemed to take on new life, and the devastating drought is over!

* * *

January 19, 1984

Graham: "You know what, Mom? I decided today in business class (at Belmont College) that the root of all the trouble in the world is greed!"

* * *

The sun is shining again at midday.

This morning I looked out at daffodils emerging unsteadily into a world in which they seem to have lost confidence! Last night they were covered with a blanket of snow!

* * *

April 14

Observation from yesterday:

Yesterday, I entertained two friends in the midday when the sun was at its zenith and the spring was at its brightest. The purpose was to show them the wildflowers in these hills and on the spring-infested hillside. In all of the surrounding beauty I found a surprising lack of excitement in the very things which had stirred my "insides" on my early morning walk. Conclusions: (after a little random thinking):

The shadows of life, both early and late, give it the essence of its meaning; the brightest midday when things are most visible puts one into a less-caring, less appreciative frame of mind.

Childhood with its "growing pains," adolescence with its struggles, and young adulthood with its stirring to make a place for itself in the world, lead to a period of midday brightness which really blinds one to the more meaningful elements of life.

When one starts his decline of years at middle age and heads himself toward the "last of life for which the first was made" the shadows once again sweep across the landscape from the passing clouds, and one sees living things in a more acute sense of the word, if he will.

As the shadows lengthen, the grass seems greener in those areas upon which they fall. The greenery still bathed in sunlight takes on a grander brightness, and one enjoys a walk from its warmth into the coolness of the shade. Maybe I don't dread growing old as much as I thought I would - maybe!

Perhaps, if I allow myself, I shall begin to enjoy little things more, notice them more frequently, relish them for longer periods as I have more spare time. Maybe it is really true that the secrets of life lie on the "other side" of the vale, and one's old age is truly but another stepping stone toward complete understanding and assimilated appreciation of all one's experiences heretofore. "Heaven," as anticipated by man through the ages in one interpretation or another, may be a fundamental and inescapable reality.

My present aim:

To allow myself as much leeway as I can muster to understand, appreciate and enjoy what is left of life at this point and to be of as much help to those coming after me as I can so that they, too, may find life's elixirs for themselves.

* * *

April 14

This was Elizabeth's thirtieth birthday! I celebrated by going on a wildflower tour of Warner Park.

The weather was certainly "questionable" when the day began. It was raining a bit, and there was no hint that the sun would shine. At 8:30 the clouds were boiling overhead, but by the time I had brought out my raincoat and put on my warm jacket, the sun was shining! As I walked to Charlotte's for my ride to the park, things began to dry out, the wind blowing ever so gently, and I felt confident that leaving my raincoat at home was going to be a secure move.

At the wildflower station house at the convergence of Old Hickory Boulevard and Highway 100 in Warner Park, we were greeted by masses of daffodils and quite a few tulips, all of the very cultivated variety, but there the cultivation stopped, except for a wildflower bed which had been laid out with old crossties to contain certain varieties.

Inside the house where the tour began, the guide had made "bush tea." It was steaming in a pot on the stove, and one of the girls ladled it out for those who wished to try it. It was made of twigs from the "spice bush." There was a basket of freshly made bread, sliced to perfection, which the mother of one of the guides had made for the occasion. To go with it, there was a jar of <u>violet</u> jelly, its hue so delicate and pink one could almost smell the violets themselves. Beside the jelly there was a small basket of cracked black walnuts to be spread on the jellied bread. What a surprise that combination was to the palate! I must try that culinary treat again. The walnut meats gave a quality of rich butter to the eating.

In the wildflower bed outside, we saw Virginia bluebells, just beginning to bloom fully. The buds were a deep pink, but they would later open into bells of the purest, strong blue. There was a patch of low-lying Nashville mustard, in full yellow, creeping about two or three inches high along the ground. It is called

"Nashville" because this is the only place in the world that this form of mustard grows.

* * *

After Graham had been on stage and sung for an audience the first time at "Senior Variety Show" rehearsals, he let me know what a wonderful feeling it was being on stage and hearing their applause.

Mother-like, I cautioned him that it was all right to like it, but that it shouldn't become too important to be on stage to be applauded!

"You miss the whole point, Mother. What I like is to be able to make people listening to me _feel_ like responding to my songs. It's what I make _them_ feel that is important!"

* * *

Dilemma of a Rainy April Afternoon

Whether to take advantage of heightened sensitivity and compulsion "to be about something" by creating something to leave behind (in the face of certain, eventual cessation of being in my present form) _or_ to stand quietly, pensively and receptively while I absorb as much as I possibly can of the wondrous beauty in the panorama before me so that I can "take it with me!" To have recorded this thought gave a little sense of the satisfaction of leaving something of myself behind; now, back to press my nose against the window pane and just simply look and listen and <u>enjoy</u>, <u>enjoy</u>!

* * *

Rain in the hills falling in a mist so nearly like fog it makes the <u>sound</u> of it <u>collectively</u> hitting the tin gutter seem shocking and detached from the truth (actuality).

* * *

Today I've made a decision, a small one it is true, but in all the course of living nothing excites me as much as the awareness of <u>positive action before</u> me. <u>That</u> must be the <u>feeling</u> that comes to a great general in time of crisis, a physician observing the revelation of the scalpel, the composer in recording a melody, the artist in preparation for application of a brush stoke, the farmer in harvesting time, <u>and</u> in truth, that moment of <u>every</u> man when he needs to realize his raison d'être!

It is the <u>potential energy</u> that gives rise to <u>force</u>.

* * *

July 4

I guess I'm really liberated today! I'm not too sure of how that makes me feel, but I can rationalize. That is the beauty of being mankind; it separates him from other animals.

George has gone to the "Board of Directors," and Graham has gone to Springfield with Danielle to visit her grandparents. I do not know what the other children are doing. Elizabeth is in Franklin, Martha Sills in Dallas and James in Auburn. My hope is that as each pursues his own thing, it will be safe and happy and rewarding. As free as I want them to be, perhaps they will give George and me a fleeting thought on this family holiday; if not, perhaps our influence will be there with them in some word or deed. We did love them so much and try to guide them the best that we knew how.

I am trying to take advantage of the realization that I am, at last, for all intents and purposes, free to get on with the things I have longed to do. Nothing is really stopping me from the painting, writing, sewing, thinking, etc., which I have longed to do. I have no real excuse. . . except the cooking and washing and cleaning. I shall try not to let those disciplines of everyday living prevent me from finding time to do things I really want to do!

The day is warm and sunny, but there is a hint of afternoon showers to come. I can't determine just what it is. . . perhaps a bit of a blueness mixed with sunshine. Whatever the mystery, it comes and goes like the shadows and breezes.

I looked out the bedroom window at the front of the house. An overwhelming greenness enveloped me and separated itself into bits of difference because of the individual trees and bushes. The tiny red stems of the maple looked as if they had been drawn in pencil to support the shapely, tipped leaves. A stirring of the summer air ruffled the leaves, caused branches to dip up and down in their swaying response, and the tops of the slender trees went 'round in a kind of circular motion. A breeze was indeed passing through, and it gave life to all of the surrounding greenery.

A young squirrel scampered across the graveled driveway, racing with the green pear he had just pilfered from the overloaded tree on the lower lawn. A pear tree is of itself a noble-looking piece of sculpture. Its limbs swirl and droop in utter grace, and when laden with its fruit, that grace becomes a beauty of sheer helplessness, like the loveliness of a child's face reflecting the innocence of a happy smile. . . Race on, little squirrel; I would not take from you your prize, or the sense of excitement that you must feel at having stolen from life's treasure house! I am the only one who sees you, unless it is the robin red breast who has been hopping a few steps here, a few steps there, about the grass, stopping every few seconds to dart to the right and left. The thing he seeks is probably an insect; the ground is too hard to yield its earthworms to him there.

Lunch is over, and drowsiness sets in. The blue haze of morning has given way to a grey-dull stillness. As is the wont of a summer shower, it began its rat-tat-tat on the roof just after noon; the morning zephyrs grew stronger, and the rains swept through. Great relief, a summer rainstorm! it sets one free from reality and into dream. I shall put my head on pillow and relish that charm of the day.

Wimbledon matches are on television. It brings back the Fourth of July, 1982! I can hardly believe Elizabeth and I were then on the River Cam at Cambridge, punting past the copper beeches and underneath the Bridge of Sighs. Humbling, funny experience. . . and then there were the narrow streets of the city; Kings' College Chapel with its exquisite colored panes; shop windows and emblemed ties; flowered gardens and ancient stone walls with "flowers in their crannied nooks!" On my breast I wore a red, white and blue cut-glass American flag, and around my throat I wore a scarf in those same colors! As we tiredly crossed Jesus Green on the way back to our bus for London, a small jazz band was seated there playing songs of Cole Porter! Fond memory, especially of the pastry I bought from a street vendor to munch on with my cup of tea.

George and I luxuriated together while watching the tennis match between Conners and the "boy from University of Tennessee . . . Anaconda." The love and closeness of a mate are ever what it's all about!

* * *

February 5

The temperatures, this morning, are high enough to start the snows of the last weeks melting. A misty kind of fog is rising, and all the out of doors seems to be adding a bit of grey from nature's palette. I realize how much it has meant to me to be separated from the hustle and bustle of contemporary life and its pressures. I feel much restored, and an experience I had on the telephone with Mother this morning was a sort of pinnacle for that respite.

Mother answered the phone from a kind of drowsiness brought on by reading and a nap into which she had fallen while sitting in her reclining chair. As we went along, she became more and more enthusiastic in telling me about events in her life during the last weeks.

"Yesterday," she said, "the sun was shining. It was a pretty day, and the bluebirds were going in and out of their nest. I read a lot and watched the bluebirds. They never could seem to find the food we had put out for them, but they were very busy going in and out of their house, anyway."

One day, a week or so ago, she had hurt her foot. There was quite a lot of bleeding. Roger was very solicitous of how she felt and wanted to take her to the doctor, but she thought she would be all right. After he left for work, not too long, T.O. Nelms showed up, all dressed up, and offered to take her to the doctor. Roger had alerted him to her condition on his way to work. She declined because she felt some better. Then in the afternoon, T.O. came <u>again</u> to see about her. She much appreciated his coming and thought it was the work of the Lord, that there must be some lack in T.O.'s life that she could have some influence over. It was to her God's way of giving her an opportunity to mean something to T.O.

Of the evils of the times she said, "All over the world people are doing whatever they want to for prestige and power." She said that in her lifetime, these are the most evil-seeming days, fulfilling Biblical prophecy, that God's chosen people have made him ashamed, but that they will eventually join hands with the Christians to become one with God.

She told me how much she loved and enjoyed the picture of Aunt Winnie and her as little girls, which I painted for her for Christmas. "One morning last week I looked at that picture, and it took me right back to those times. It was so real, I decided to sit down at the organ and play some of Winnie's favorite hymns. I sat there and played through the whole book, ending with 'I'll Meet You in the Morning.' It was a wonderful experience. I cried and cried sweet tears of release. Then I read Bible verses I knew Winnie loved.

"Just before lunch, Marjorie came in from Raleigh. I fixed her a good bite to eat and told her what I had just been doing. She said, after a while, 'Aunt Millie, please go in there and play me some of those hymns you just played for Aunt Winnie.' I did, and it seemed to make her very happy. She hasn't been getting along very well since Dell [her mother] died."

When I was just about to conclude our conversation, Mother said, "Charlotte, I want you to be with me some day, I really do!" She was so sweet and sincere.

I have never been able to go along with Mother's version of religion. My background of experiences does not allow me to think some of the same things. It has plagued me a good part of my life and has driven me away from religion. Today, however, after talking with mother, I prayed as I washed dishes that I could reconcile the differences in our beliefs, which I realize are not too different, but which Mother cannot accept because she sees them differently. My prayer was that I could find comfort in their <u>sameness</u>. As I raised my eyes toward the woods, I saw there a flock of beautiful doves, peacefully waiting for me to give them food on this snow-filled day. I saw it as a beautiful <u>sign</u> of reconciliation, so I went out happily to feed them!

* * *

October 29

October is about to give way to November, but she continues to mesmerize with her gentle breezes and warm sunshine as her leaves wave in the gentle caressing motion, the windsong barely audible. This year there is still much green, and some of the maples have yet to turn. Some hickories are bare, but before me there is a sweeping branch in cadmium yellow medium which waves in the breeze and occasionally lets go of a single leaf, twirling to the ground. Already there is a crunchy brown carpet underneath the large trees which last week shed their autumn finery. Evergreens are waxy in the sunlight, and a bright red cardinal is sitting among the dark green holly branches. Soon these two will afford all of the true color, except for blue skies, but today the dogwoods are reddening, and the beeches and maples are yellowing fast. In three days, November will be here.

Yesterday we returned from an annual pilgrimage home to North Carolina. This year's trip fulfilled all of the emotional vacancies of my heart, and I am spiritually renewed, it seems.

George and I left Nashville at 6:45 a.m. two weeks ago under grey skies and slightly falling rain. How pleasant it was to travel east and not to stare into the upcoming sun in early morning hours. Many trees were already in their full colors, but summer green was more prevalent, accented with the affluent evergreen of Tennessee cedar trees dotting the landscape, clinging to the edges of the fields and pasturelands. We rode in silence ourselves, the local "Music of Your Life" radio station playing sentimental songs which evoked both separate and joint memories for each of us. Down the highways of Tennessee and over the mountains into North Carolina we went, a trip we've made so many dozens of times, to join our present life to our past and bring home a feeling of love renewed.

* * *

April

On a recent trip to the hospital, my mother, Millie, was extremely weak after a bout with a migraine headache and a prolonged period of breaking out on her legs, which the doctor was not able to diagnose. Some people from her church carried her directly to Louisburg Hospital on Sunday afternoon. She was put in the room with an old acquaintance with whom she had been in the hospital before.

In the early morning Monday, the old lady, mother's friend, died right there in the room. Danny was upset that Mother should have had to undergo such a bad experience, but in her gentle, quiet way, Mother told her not to worry, she would be able, with God's help, to bear the experience. . .

Monday night another acquaintance, Mrs. White, was moved in with Mother. She was very old and very sick and did not even know who she was or where she was. She kept falling off the bed during the night and the next morning. One time, she got up and fell into the wastebasket. Mother would try to get out of bed and help poor Mrs. White. Now, one would wonder why the staff didn't put railings or some kind of restraint so that poor Mrs. White would not keep having those problems. They did not, so Mother continued to try to help her. . .

About 11:00 this morning, Tuesday, Dr. Perry came in to see Mother. He found her weeping. "Miss Millie, what on earth is wrong with you?" he asked.

"Oh, Dr. Perry," Mother said through her tears, "I'm just too weak to take care of Mrs. White. It is just too much responsibility for me in this condition!" So Dr. Perry had Mother moved to a private room where she regained her strength, and was released from the hospital about a week later. . .

This is a good example of how responsible for other people the family always was; how our parents were, themselves, and how we are inside, and how we have brought our children up to be. "Doing something for someone else" was the backbone of our existence.

* * *

June 23, James's birthday

On Thinking of James and Graham in Their Teenage Years

What does it matter that your sons look foreign to your eye?

Fall Colors

That they care not for the things which mean the most
to you?

You did not, on purpose, make an effort to sublimate
them to your own ways.

The life you gave them, through the grace of God,

Was theirs to explore and to harness, as best they
could,

In communion with the will of the Almighty, one has
fervently prayed.

How can you have suffered so in watching the
diversities

And alienations they have exhibited?

Have you loved them less or more?

Has the advice you've given, both lovingly and in
despair, fallen on deaf

Or more resentful ears?

Would a warm and understanding smile of
appreciation make things well?

Or does the loving heart of a mother seek a ray of
gratitude that it does not,

Yet hopes to, deserve?

Surely her love, which was born of personal desire,

Hovered around her growing infants,

Extended into contemporary realms of which she had
no understanding,

And for which she feels no kinship,

And strengthened by the very tensions which have knit
it together,

Must set it apart from all else

And give it infinite endurance.

Perhaps anguish, entwined with the tenderest feelings,

Gives meaning and strength to the essence of love

Between mother and child.

One sound of their dear voices erases all trace of doubt

So that I know their love for me exists

And perseveres

And pervades,

Even as does my love for them.

Charlotte B. Perry

* * *

Graham's conversation at breakfast this Saturday morning is too priceless for words, particularly in light of all of the hullabaloo in recent months about the Governor's "Master Teacher Plan" and merit raises and evaluation systems for promotion of most qualified teachers!

It is his senior year at Hillwood, and he has been working in the library this semester instead of having a study hall. As he tells it, you could tell exactly what the librarians were going to be like when he walked in to work the first day. Of the three, only one of them does all of the work, and she is <u>not</u> the head librarian, and she is much unappreciated by the other two.

It seems that two of them stand and talk, and talk, and talk. I've heard them talk about everything, but mostly they talk about kids that come storming through the library. It is always talking about things that are <u>wrong</u>. The head librarian keeps the "vertical file." It is the "worst" vertical file I've <u>ever</u> seen, according to Graham. "She never clips anything except <u>The Tennessean</u>." The one librarian who works does everything, except what the helpers do. Graham files books, and files cards and straightens up, and counts the excuse notes and checks in books and shelves books, etc.

One day this week Graham arrived in the library early. It seems that the students have seven minutes between classes, so he sat down to rest a few seconds before starting bell rang. "Shelve those books," the head librarian ordered.

"If you don't mind, I'm going to rest a minute until the bell rings," Graham said as politely as he knew how.

"Shelve those books," she demanded.

"If you don't mind, I'm going to rest a minute."

"There's no time to rest! My, my Graham is being violent today!"

"So I just got up and started to shelve the books, Mother."

The funniest thing Graham notices is that only the librarians at school seem interested in the library. They have to keep a record of everyone who comes to the library. "You ought to see how they rush to make a note of every student who enters, even if he is only walking through the library to go somewhere else!"

"Some people are favorites. If they walk through, the librarians say in a sweet, put-on way, 'Oh, how are you?' If other students come in they say, 'What are you doing in here? Get out!'"

Of the three librarians, which one would you suppose might be promoted under the "Master Teacher" plan? One dominates and criticizes and talks about everybody; one talks with her and agrees, and one works all the time at the library tasks. Graham said to the latter one day, "You do all the work!" She looked flushed, hesitated a second, then said, "It's good to be appreciated!"

The student workers do not even get any credit for their work. In essence they keep the business going from day to day. "The librarians treat us all like children who don't have any sense," Graham says, and in nearly five months, he has never seen the head librarian do anything constructive, except clip for the vertical file from the daily <u>Tennessean</u>.

I sincerely think that a student's opinion should be considered seriously, as well as a parent's, when and if teachers are "evaluated" for merit raises and master status.

* * *

May 3

Dear Graham has said for some time that he has his very own relationship with God. It does not necessarily fit into anyone else's theology, especially that of the Baptists and members of the Church of Christ, the people with whom he has been in most contact during his life here in the Bible Belt. . .

Last night I overheard him talking to Rob. "I have always subscribed to what I call 'The Trainset Philosophy of God.' Don't you?" he asked.

Obviously having been asked to verbalize on the subject, he continued, "Well, have you ever built a layout for a train set. . . trees and buildings and people and trains and stations and all that? I have built some elaborate ones, and when I was through, I just sat there on the floor beside it, and I wished and imagined that all of those things would come to life. . . that those people would take off doing things their own way while I sat and watched. Then I could have stepped in at any moment, but I didn't want to. I wanted to see what they would do for themselves. . . let them make their own mistakes and their own triumphs. . . I just sat there and loved them and believed they could do it!. . . I didn't try to interfere in my moments of imagining that they were real. I just wanted to see them do it themselves. . . Well, that's sort of the way I look at God. . . He wants us to do things for ourselves. . . He has given us everything to work with. . . and that's sort of what I call my 'Trainset Philosophy of God.'"

* * *

One day after chapel at Belmont an overly sincere fundamentalist waited for Graham and said, "Graham, I want you to know God!"

"Oh, don't worry about me! I've known God ever since I was born!"

* * *

May

The spirit of the Mildmay family creeps over me again! It couldn't have been more wonderful in 15th

- 192 -

Century England to have been Lord and Lady Mildmay themselves than to be their descendant here in Middle Tennessee in the 20th Century, surrounded by opulent green tenderness of broad-leafed hardwoods waving their spring finery, the sunlight shining above, below and through them.

I've often considered what I would leave behind me to represent the fact that I had once passed through an existence on this planet earth. Having been brought up on the theory that "all is vanity" and one should not expect to lay up treasures on earth where "moth and rust corrupt," I cannot expect to leave behind me any tangible representation. My writing is not good enough; my painting has never had time to flourish; my children sometimes curse me, and my tapestries are not too finely woven!

Shall I leave this body in assurance of Christian rewards for my soul? No matter how I strive to understand acquiescence, I cannot make the grade. I can only think that I was not "one of the chosen" as described in the New Testament (or the Old).

What then shall I leave when I depart this life? What essence may I take with me wherever my spirit goes?

On this beautiful May day I can ask no more than that I someday soar on silver wings of the memory of this morning's find in the nearby forest. As we walked down the road on Jocelyn Hollow, I glanced over my left shoulder in the direction we had just taken. A nine o'clock sunshine was bringing its life into the darkness of the early woods.

Wondrous surprise to eye, imagination and soul! There appeared in the burgeoning warmth of this May morn a patch of <u>yellow sorrel</u>! I had never seen it before, and its leaves looked like shamrocks clustered together in a fairy ring! The thrill of that sight alone has made my life spiritual! I hope to take it with me when I go!

* * *

May 19

It has been at least six weeks since we first noticed our little pair of wrens was busily building a nest inside the little hand-painted house we had hung from the eaves of our back porch. With its Pennsylvania Dutch designs, the house was still hanging by the paper ribbon which had come 'round the package when friend Tatie gave it to us last fall. I had kept intending to replace the string with something more substantial, but after it was already being prepared for occupancy by the wrens, we dared not touch the house. They worked several days bringing all kinds of materials to line the nest, even feathers from other birds! Once I saw little mother-to-be bringing a long piece of polyurethane plastic trailing after her.

Then we saw no activity for days, and we were afraid they had given up on establishing a nest there. Every once in a while, however, we'd see a wren going into the box or out of it. The weather was wet and cold.

One day about three weeks ago we saw the mother, with a worm in her mouth, fly into the nest. After that, things became more frantic, and we saw both mother and father going in and out from early morning until dusk. We were overwhelmed at the amount of work and energy it must take for the wrens to feed their family as it matured. We could hardly wait to see the babies. I kept meaning to look in the encyclopedia and find out how long we could expect it to take for the babies to get their first flying lesson. It seemed an endless period.

Today, about nine o'clock, after at least three weeks of constant feeding, I saw the mother wren in the nearby peach tree, about four yards from the nest. She was making a kind of clucking singing of four syllables. I figured she was up to something. She kept looking toward the nest, so I expected to see signs of the babies. . . that was hours ago. Then, at a little past noon, in the bright sunshine, I saw the mother wren, a worm in her mouth, fly up to the opening hole of the house, perch momentarily on the rest at the door, then take off hurriedly toward the peach tree, worm <u>still</u> in her mouth! In a minute or two the head of a baby ap-peared at the opening, beak boldly out. There it sat motionless for several minutes. All of a sudden the mother came to the handle of the lawn mower sitting on the porch, perched there a second, then gave a swift swoop past the baby bird sitting at the opening and on to the roof of our house out of sight. There was a tiny flittering darkness from the birdhouse opening, and the baby had flown past me to the direction of the peach tree! I couldn't see where it had landed! Disappointment!

Almost immediately another beak appeared at the hole in the birdhouse. Then, almost as quickly, another beak appeared. There the two sat together, waiting their turn. I could see shadows of fluttering in the peach tree area. As if impatient, another baby took off in unexpected flight. It suddenly left the ground whence it had landed and appeared on the large grey limb at the bottom of the tree, about wall-high. I could see it plainly. It looked as if it wobbled from side to side as it picked at its sides and underneath its wings for bird lice, I suppose. Several times it looked as if it would fall from its perch in the tree.

I glanced back to the birdhouse just in time to see the tiniest little creature, almost black in its brownness, fly down to the straw on the floor about a yard or so away. It just sat there on the floor for a second; then it flew a yard away to land on the freshly painted green leg of George's chair. It clung sideways for a few seconds before it flew toward the post of the porch. Oops! That was too big and too smooth, and there was nothing to cling to on its side. The baby practically slid down to the porch floor! There it sat and sat and sat and sat. The mother and the father wrens were so engaged with teaching their first two babies about the outside world in the peach tree they seemed to have forgotten this middle child!

In the meantime, back at the door of the birdhouse, the baby was getting ideas. Fast! It couldn't wait for the other children, so it flew down to the top of the lawn mower handle and sat watching its middle sibling wait to get waited on! The middle child, still unat-

Tulips and Dogwood

tended, hopped down to the ground, played around a few seconds, and then was joined by its mother, who sat beside it momentarily, then flew back to the peach tree. The baby followed almost immediately. It had been just waiting for that word of encouragement!

The baby by this time had really gotten impatient. It flew down to the straw and sat there briefly. The mother and father and the other babies had, by this time, taken off toward the woods. The baby didn't wait on ceremony. It flew in a longish flight <u>past</u> the peach tree and directly to the stone wall. Sitting there long enough to take in what was going on with his family, he took off after them, landing near his mother at the edge of the woods, quite a distance away! I saw them both hopping around for a few seconds, then they disappeared into the shadows of the trees.

I could hear some new noises coming from that direction. They sounded like crickets on a summer's evening, but I knew that they were the voices of at least four little wrens on their first outing. I really think there were five of them, but I have recorded the flight of only the ones I actually remember seeing.

The last time I noticed the peach tree a few minutes ago, it was the perching place for a sparrow and the little half-grown peaches were quietly awaiting the time of maturation and ripening in their own lifecycle. Life moves forward steadily, and patience is required of every living thing. The wrens were not to be seen. We wonder if they will return to their house to sleep tonight, or if they will camp out in the open, not to return until someone goes back, in time, to the homestead for another nesting. We'll be on the lookout.

* * *

PUDDIN' -- DEAR LITTLE YORKIE

It is absolutely impossible to fathom the reason or the depth of one's affection for his pet, and a very small creature, a Yorkshire terrier, has just passed through my life in a reasonably brief span, but leaving a swath of emptiness that seems at the moment without bounds.

Puddin' belonged to Elizabeth, my beloved oldest child. She made her bid for a place in Elizabeth's heart with a wistful look from a pen in Jones's Pet Shop on Hillsboro Road on the occasion of Elizabeth's 21st birthday. Half of her purchase price was my birthday present to Elizabeth, and the size of the bill would have made an almost complete covering for the tiny creature which she brought home that day. The name Puddin' was a not-too-imaginative designation, but in our minds it was our only association with Yorkshire, and it definitely seemed to fit the dear, petite, wobbly six-week old puppy with the too big, too brown, deeply cognitive eyes, who melted your heart like butter on warm bread, immediately.

From the beginning Puddin' was just not truly healthy, and it was very difficult to find anything that she would eat. Trips to the vet, grocery and canine-loving friends produced much advice, but little help in finding anything that Puddin' would eat. She seemed to survive on coaxing and good, heartfelt, pleading, wishes and a little cottage cheese, a bit of milk, and a few drops of honey. Perhaps her greatest challenge for the next four years and a few months was finding something for her to eat. She had low blood sugar and spells of trembling to correspond with it, off and on, always. It was not until the last few months of her life that I found out that I could forestall most of her troubles of this kind by being very firm and forcing her to eat a tablespoon of honey, scooped, a bit at a time, onto my index finger and rubbed on the outside of her mouth so that she was forced to lick it off. When she had had enough, she would wiggle and squirm like a willful child to get out of my arms, and shortly there-after she would eat other food.

At breakfast I fixed one slice of bacon especially for Puddin'. This I crumbled over her softly scrambled egg (a portion taken from George and James's breakfast before it was completely cooked). If the bacon were of top quality, she would devour it with great relish, then prance off back to her box in the bedroom to sleep for a while, or sometimes lie quietly by the vent of the refrigerator where the heat from the motor flowed through onto the floor in the kitchen. (Inferior quality bacon she simply would not touch.) In fact, her hours lying by this vent were endless while I cooked the meals for the family. She would look up at me occasionally, and I often rubbed her gently with my foot when I went to put something in the icebox. I always hated to disturb her by putting things in the freezer and was so gentle in the process that she finally learned not to go away when I opened the door, but merely to move a bit.

It was finally established fact that Puddin' would not eat an inexpensive brand of bacon. She would simply go to her saucer, take a sniff and walk quietly, disappointedly out of the room. She did, however, like "salt" bacon when I fixed it for George. She would eat one food for a few weeks, then it would be unaccep-table from then on. She had binges of cottage cheese, ham thinly sliced, green peas, butterbeans, bologna, homemade soup, etc., but she never ate dog food except for an occasional nibble of Ken'l Ration from Cub's bowl. Once or twice she nearly killed herself by overturning the kitchen garbage bag during the night for a chicken bone or some ham fat which had been thrown away. . . Such forages were frightening to us and the cause of great discomfort to Puddin'. I think it was the challenge of getting into the bag that intrigued her. Had I left a chicken bone on the floor for her as I often did a beef bone, she would not have touched it!

It is not possible to preserve Puddin' by written word on a piece of mere paper. My loving thoughts will not shape themselves into words, and my thoughts and memories of that dear little black and tan Yorkie go fleeting here and there, to and fro, in such vocal sequence and with such rapidity, I am reminded of an electronic scanner reacting to the slightest provo-cation. When I am successful in steadying one of these recollections of that dear little dog, I mostly see a soft, minute bundle of love cradled briefly in my left arm, her perching there, more often than not, seeming only a temporary retreat until she could catch some object of interest, begin her struggle for freedom, then plunge after it in a kind of happy-puppy canter! I would run breathlessly after her down the street until she found a reason to stop and explore. . .

The joy of Puddin's last months at my house was her nightly romp down Rolling Fork Drive to the intersection with Jocelyn Hollow. She had made friends with every dog along the street, and because of her minute appearance she seemed quite a curiosity to most of them. There was only one spoiled dachshund on a leash that shied away from her curious inspective friendship as if in fear. Otherwise, she was always making friends. She was inately gregarious with other dogs! Her first stop after leaving our driveway was in the Cain's yard for a sneak visit with Buffy, the Chesapeake Bay Retriever. Then we proceeded at <u>her</u> will down the street. About halfway, a mixed sort of German Shepherd - Collie named Pabst joined us every night. He would sniff lovingly at Puddin', who enjoyed his attention thoroughly, but when weary of too much interference, she would snap at that great big giant in a snippishly feminine way, and off they would both go down the street. Pabst was so protective of us for the rest of the mile that he actually would fight another dog that came to close to us. One night our own dog, Cub, escaped and came to join us. Pabst fought him three times, rather violently, because he came near us. I was helpless to stop the altercation, so protective he was of Puddin'.

I can't explain without seeming foolish how intelligent and how cognitive of her surroundings Puddin' was. She could tell which door I was going to exit by what I had in my hands. The pocketbook and regular things let her know that I was leaving via the front door, and she escaped with lightning movements to run to my car and wait hopefully for a ride as often as she could manage. When it was time to take Graham to school in the early morning, she was always ready and exhibiting that full-potential energy waiting by the front door when the time of departure came. If she went with us, she licked the steering wheel all the way there and back, or some times substituted my hands. . . When I took a bag of garbage into the same hallway, Puddin' went immediately to the back door, because that is the route I took. The miles she paddled around behind me in this house are endless, and if I wanted to be sure that she could not get to things like Graham's train tracks, etc., to explore dangerous things, I had to shut each door behind me, being very careful that she did not scoot through the door ahead of me, so fast in fact that I would not even see her.

Once when Elizabeth and Puddin' were living here in the house before Elizabeth's marriage, Puddin' stopped eating. She finally became sick unto death, it seemed. Elizabeth took her to the emergency pet clinic twice one Sunday, but there seemed to be nothing to do for her. On Monday morning when she went to work, I took the dying puppy to Dr. Clauton and left her, hoping that they could somehow find a way to help her. At two o'clock in the afternoon, when I went back to check on her, I found a much amused and querulous doctor and a much improved little dog, though still shaking with fright. Dr. Clauton reached into his pocket, withdrew a little medication envelope and emptied into his hand a little length of metal with a bead on the end. "Mrs. Perry," he asked in his lisping manner, "have you ever seen 'thsis' before?"

I had to admit that I had never seen that little ornament, although it did look as if it might have come from a piece of jewelry.

"Well, take 'thsis' home and please see if anyone recognizes it. If you can find out what it is, I'd like to know. I've removed over 25 hundred things from dogs' stomachs and intestines before, but I've never seen anything like 'thsis'. If you will bring it back to me for my collection later, I will appreciate it." he then showed me the oversized x-ray of that little dog, which revealed the trinket in the lower intestine. . . The dog, having had the object removed, was a bit shaken, but fine, and I took her bundled up in a towel to the car to go to pick Graham up from school.

When Graham came to the car to go home, I pulled the little packet out, removed the trinket and asked, "Graham, have you ever seen this before?"

He grinned sheepishly and said, "Yes."

"What is it?"

"It is the part of my Confederate cannon that shoots the projectile out!"

We knew thereafter to keep Puddin' away from the miniature Civil War battlefield in Graham's room. . . but I have a hunch that, through the years, she probably found things in her explorations that were hardly more palatable. She just managed to keep them from getting so nearly permanently lodged!

Puddin' was a "one-man" dog all her life until the last few months. She loved Elizabeth with a passion that made her sick when they separated. It took nearly the whole time of Elizabeth's stay in Atlanta in paralegal school for Puddin' to come around, although she was very dependent upon us and very close. She learned to like George then and often begged to get in his lap. She would lie on his stomach while he read the evening paper, perched like a lion on the steps of a public library.

But when Elizabeth was around, there was simply nobody else in the whole world! Puddin' pranced behind Elizabeth when she went from one room to another, her short tail with the minute curl at its tip proudly raised, as she followed like a Lilliputian pony in a race at Ascot. You could hear the rapid little footfalls all the way down the hall, and you could feel the satisfaction that came with Elizabeth's picking her up for a loving hold. She would lie in bed beside her in blissful satisfaction as Elizabeth worked her needlepoint or crewel work and watched TV. Puddin' followed at Elizabeth's heels for her every move. . .

But after Elizabeth and Dave were married and she had to go to work every day, leaving Puddin' alone in the apartment, with the problem of feeding her early in the morning during her palsied trembling and low blood sugar periods, it was obvious that the dog could not live without something special being done for her. She stopped eating almost altogether, and we decided that the humane thing was to have her put to sleep. With tears and much sorrow, Elizabeth asked me to have something done. I promised and went sadly to pick her up. The doctor agreed that it was probably best for us all, and I promised to bring her in to him when I could bring myself around to doing so. . . I couldn't do it.

Those big brown, sad eyes followed me everywhere, and she lay there in the warmth of the refrigerator exhaust, trembling and helpless. My heartstrings were so stirred, and my frustration was so nearly complete, that in desperation I noticed the "squirt" water bottle one of the boys had used in an athletic program. I warmed some milk, melted some honey and added a bit of raw egg to the mixture. Cradling Puddin' in my left arm, I proceeded to squirt a bit of that nourishment into her mouth, a bit at the time from the plastic bottle. Her little pink tongue lapped greedily at it. I let her rest, then continued the feeding.

After half an hour or so, she was up, standing by the door, looking longingly at the thing as if she wanted desperately to go outside. When I opened it, she was off like a flitting little black shadow, and I had a hard time keeping up with her down the drive. That began what turned out to be the joy of her life, our walks down Rolling Fork! Thereafter she alternately pranced like a little racehorse, stopped to sniff at some blade of grass which bore the scent of another dog, and paused to leave her own 'calling card" by daintily lifting her right leg forward (the latter process which much amused George).

At first she could not make it halfway down the street before giving out. At that point, I would pick her up and carry her perched softly in the crook of my left arm. She weighed no more than four pounds even when she had regained her appetite and we considered her absolutely "fat." From March until July 11 we made hundreds of treks down the street and sometimes up the street toward the hills. She explored and cantered to her little heart's content, and I loved her more and more.

When I took a nap on the sofa, she slept in a soft, warm, contented cuddle beside me. She knocked and pawed at the bedroom door, begging to be let inside. Then she whined to get on the bed with me and go to sleep. Her presence was as conducive to relaxation and rest as a snifter of fine brandy or a potent sleeping pill. Being there, she seemed to say always, "I _need_ you and I _enjoy_ being with you."

On the evening of July 11, the TV program "Tic Tac Dough" was just over. Mark and Graham went to Jeanette's car to get her suitcase for her. The end of the program was always a signal for Puddin' that it was time to go for her evening walk. Every day she became truly excited when that program came on because she knew it was almost time to go outside. When the boys went out, I heard that the door was not completely closed, so I got up immediately as I heard Puddin' push it open and rush excitedly after them. I made my move to go after her, realizing that she might take off down the drive alone, but I was too late. In less than a minute I went outside and there I met the boys with Puddin' in Graham's arms, still and warm, but not breathing. I absolutely panicked! I knew she was badly hurt.

As Graham had closed the door of the car, not hard, just routinely, Puddin' had jumped up trying to get inside. She must have snapped her neck, thin little source of life that it was. I lost all my senses and left the emergency up to everyone else. I begged James to call the Emergency Pet Clinic. Together we tried to find a place open, and we did. It was just 7:30 then. A few minutes made such a difference! Jeanette tried to massage her heart, but she felt it give its last quiver. She knew it was too late. The boys knew it was over, but they all tried to salve my feelings, and George, Mark and Graham took off with Puddin' down the street, in the car, headed for help. . . to Dr.

Clauton's, to the clinic, they didn't know where, just anything to seek help for that darling little dog. Within minutes they came back up the drive, and when I saw them coming, I knew it was hopelessly over.

It all happened so quickly, and I felt so wretched, so sad! I wanted to hold her again and feel her soft little loving body, but I didn't want to touch her dead! On the brick steps by the dogwood tree leading to the front door I decided that holding her again was a must. Graham handed her gently to me, cradling her limp little form, and I held her for the last time. She was still warm and soft, and her little fat stomach looked so sweet. She had eaten such a good supper of my homemade vegetable soup.

How glad I was I had fed her before I sat down for my own. Her comfort, as usual, came before mine. After a minute of loving her lifeless body, I went inside to find an appropriate something to wrap her in for burial. Lying on the bathroom vanity was a lovely old linen hand towel which Mama Jenny had made years ago. It had handmade fringe and a feel of quality. I picked it up, went outside and once more picked Puddin' up, laid her gently onto its smoothness and gave her a last loving look. She was peaceful and quiet in contrast to her joyful exuberance of twenty-five minutes before. Her big brown eyes were only half closed, but they were no longer looking at me. They seemed to say that I was no longer needed. It was painful to accept after all of the pleading looks of need she had given me so many times.

I brushed the forelock of her hair forward in the Yorkie tradition, but as I did I remembered the playful pawing, with both petite, delicate paws, at it that she had so often done, as if trying to rearrange it to clear her view; so, I gently brushed part of it back. Then I quickly folded the fine linen towel smoothly over her, picked her up carefully while supporting her neck and handed her to Graham. I had seen that little bit of loving Yorkie for the last time.

George said we needed to place her in the edge of the woods, not in the yard. So I chose a spot near the lovely yellow maples at the corner, a place that we could see, but not obviously so. It was painful to choose a box for her. The trade names on shoeboxes didn't seem to fit - Adidas, Grasshoppers, Delisos, etc. Graham found a Rudy's Farm box that was just the right size, and being that the Rudys have meant so much to us all, it was exactly right in every way. George and the boys alternately dug and cut away at the roots of trees and the hard rocky soil.

I, myself, put the soil over the box and our sleeping doggie. Then with strenuous effort, George and Graham tugged and rolled the large concrete slab, taken from Darlene and Rusty's brick wall to the hillside and placed it on top of the little grave, a protection and mark of haven for Puddin'. Later, I picked a few daisies, snapdragons, passion flower blossoms, sweet peas, Queen Ann's Lace and pink yarrow, which I made into a little nosegay. This final token, I placed on the top of the slab has lain there for more than a week now. My heart has truly ached, but like the fading flowers, the freshness of the hurt is ebbing. Replacing the sudden sting of pain is a sort of pleasant memory that flits through my thoughts and haunts my vision of the things that I associate with the dearest, sweetest little animal I've ever known. Puddin', the dearest, sweetest little animal I've ever known. Puddin', Elizabeth's Yorkshire Terrier, a love that I shall treasure forever!

* * *

There were four other dogs which made our home and family theirs on Rolling Fork.

First of all, Phillip the basset hound was given to Elizabeth by Carl Gardner, a friend of George's who wanted to make the children welcomed to Nashville to live. Carl let George and the children come to his home on Old Hickory Boulevard to see the whole new litter of puppies and take their pick. One, of course, stole their hearts, and they named him "Phillip" for their ancestor Phillip III of France, about whom Mother had already told them. Phillip was a perfect pet - gentle, lovable and beautifully long-eared. We though he could do no wrong - and when the next door neighbor said he was getting into her garbage can, we denied that the short-legged dog could even reach the top of her can to rob it. Then - one night there was a mighty clanging at our front door, and when it was opened, there was Phillip, his head poked through the garbage can lid, ears and all! He looked like a Shakespearean actor ready for the show to go on. The expression on his face was one of as much perplexity as the faxes we wore on finding him thus attired!

James loved sitting beside Phillip on the back porch while rubbing his ears. This seemed a perfect way for an active four-year-old boy to rest before his next venture. The artist-mother in me surged forth, and the first ambitious oil painting I undertook was one of James, with Phillip resting at his young master's feet.

The next dog to enter our lives at 6604 Rolling Fork was Cub, and he came to meet the family in James's arms on Thanksgiving day. Grandmother and Grandfather Jennings were visiting, so the dinner-time was a little more prolonged and formal than usual. James asked to be excused from the table and ran over to play with his friend Craig. Soon they appeared at our table with an armful of fluffy, adorable puppy. For Grandmother it was love at first sight! "May I keep him, Mother?" was the next question, and the answer could only be, "Yes." Cub soon roamed the neighborhood with the boys and lived a mutually happy life.

[Here the author intended to include a paragraph about Stonewall]

Bear was a birthday present to Graham, and he came over the mountains from North Carolina with George and me. He was six weeks old, a ball of auburn fur surrounding a precious face with a purple tongue. We all took him into heart, and Stonewall became his lord protector. In order to relieve any fears of friends who had a built-in fear of chows, I always took Bear to the kitchen with me when I was serving guests. He retreated to his bowl of water and food each time and eventually took his banishment from the assembled company in the living room as a sign that his water and food needed to be defended. Thereafter, I did not need to tell my guests that I'd rather not have them help me in the kitchen. Bear's formidable growl was enough!

After his walk with George and his perusal of the neighborhood, Bear took his place on the front hillside as sentinel of the homestead. He was our sign of best defense for a <u>long</u> time!

* * *

May 2

Today I watched a 1940's old black and white movie. It was about the <u>Fighting Sullivans</u>, five boys who had enlisted together in the U. S. Navy and had gone down on the same ship during WWI. It was a true story, and it set me to thinking about those days. . .

This being a dark, rainy afternoon, the movie's being without color, I tend to think in terms of dreary color. Today we are so used to color television, color at its height in movies, materials available in every conceivable hue for clothing, upholstery, house furnishings, etc. Could it be that today is brighter than were the old days. . . or were they as bright, only we didn't have technical equipment in the form of cameras to catch them and record their vivacity? Surely trees were as tender and green in the springtime then; I specifically remember one warmish spring day when, as a small child, I went to my grandmother's house to spend the afternoon. The hickory trees were leaved in such supple and yellow green, and they were full of cascading green blooms blowing gracefully in the breeze. Yes, that is one memory I have of the past that maintains its color in my mind - pale, new hickory leaf green. But the days of WWII! Were they colorful? Right now I tend to think of them in a haze.

I remember when I heard about Pearl Harbor. . . late on a grey December Sunday afternoon, which I had spent at my Grandmother Braswell's. I remember everything perfectly about Daddy's turning on the radio in the dusk, and the news! The stunning news! But I recall no color at all in that picture, only perhaps the brown radio!

Daddy drove a blue Fork at the time. . . the blue of it comes back as one of heightened intensity, but really rather blank compared with a blue Ford of today. I had that year a beautiful plaid skirt of maroon and appropriately muted contrasting colors. There must have been a blue thread in it though; I wore a pale blue sweater with it. The paleness of that blue I can

Bear

recall; the rest of that year seems colorless except for the gold and royal blue of the school basketball uniforms and the satin ribbons which bore out the school theme for the Junior-Senior Banquet. I do remember the pretty green chiffon evening dress I wore. It was apple green, and I used a pink lace hand-kerchief with it. The latter was an idea of Hilda Denton and Mother, and someone gave me pink carnations to wear with it. It must have been Lynn Williams, or was it really Mother and Hilda? I can't remember!

In those years, the most colorful thing I remember, I suppose, was Gone With the Wind. It was a shockingly beautiful movie, and we all remarked about its being in "Technicolor." Surely it was the most colorful thing any of us had ever witnessed!

People bought black cars, or grey cars or white cars or brown cars in those days. Herbert Scoggin, in Louisburg, had a red convertible with a white top. All of us who hoped to own a car of our own some day hoped to have a dark red convertible, too. Maybe Detroit was putting out colorful autos then, but not many people around our parts were purchasing them. . . I do remember way back in 1929 when my sister was born that Doctor Denton had a light green

Chevrolet coupe with chromium-looking Hogarth-like curves adorning the top of its body. But most of the cars of my childhood were not notably colorful. . . Oh, but I do remember Uncle Bill's Hudson. It was a magnificent royal blue with a black top and with grey plush insides.

People in my growing-up years usually painted inside their houses in pale blue, pink, green or yellow with woodwork trimmed in white. Most of the wall-papers I remember were in pale floral colors. Living room "suites" were more often than not in browns, perhaps with floral designs cut into their velour and outlined in a maroon or very dark color. When people began to slipcover overstuffed sofas, things became more alive and fresh.

I remember the most colorful piece of clothing of all in my childhood seemed to be my Uncle Bobby's yellow slicker, which he would wear home from college - Wake Forest. Everything else seems to be white shirts and dark britches for the men I knew. . . unless it were a blue serge suit or a grey pin stripe! I do remember Aunt Marguerite's navy blue georgette dress which had a yoke underlain with pink, and I remember Mother's getting dressed for church once in a white picture hat, wearing a while silk dress, carrying a bouquet of white peonies. . . not very colorful, but a very stunning picture for a child to carry in her mind forever, especially since my mother had such black hair that I later noticed it had navy blue highlights! And I do remember getting ready to go to church with my grandmother when she was wearing a brownish small-figured dress with little blue specs in it. The yoke was an off-white eggshell color and she made a great to-do about draping her two-foot-long strand of blue glass beads around her throat.

It was such a nice sight, I in later years asked her if I might have those beads, and she gave them to me for my birthday. I still love to take them out and let the sunlight catch in their blueness. Only they aren't as bright and sparkling in reality as they seemed to me then; dust has lodged in their crevices, and the cut of the glass design is not very sharp, but oh, how I love those beads, and how precious the memory of my Grannanny Boone as she was getting ready to go to Belford Church on that special Sunday morning! The rest of her clothes I remember as black and grey and navy blue, with matching hats. Sometimes the hats had white or pink or red cabbage roses.

The baskets of flowers she often carried with her to put on the altar were another story. I cannot only see the purple lilacs; I can almost smell them. . . the white ones, too. The iris she carried were purple, their spikes green. . . no fancy yellow or salmon colored ones. . . just purple iris in their lush, wet, fragile watery tenderness. The roses were either white or pink; I do not remember any red ones except the moss rose with the finely, thickly-thorned stems. But the lemon lilies were of the dearest buttery yellow, and their fragrance was as subtle and lovely as their color. None of them was ever a match for today's highly developed, crossbred, hothouse varieties of lily, but their imprint on the memory is as clear and as precious.

I cannot leave customs I remember without mentioning dear, great, great Aunt Ella Williams Sills. When I was in first or second grade, she came to visit. It is the only time I ever remember having seen her. She must have stayed a week or so at my grand-mother's. During that time my mother entered me in a so-called "Beauty Contest." It was held at Edward Best High School, and I was then attending Cedar Rock Elementary School (formerly Cedar Rock Academy). Mother dressed me in a bright pink dress of satin, which was made with two eight or ten-inch puffed sleeves. She brought me to my grandmother's house to dress me and send me off to the event in the family car, which we all shared.

I can remember now the color of my dress, and I can feel the pink of my cheeks, although I could not see them; my mother had heightened the color in them with a little of her rouge so I would look appealing from the stage to the audience! When she completed dressing me, there I stood in my grandmother's kitchen; there also stood great, great, Aunt Ella. She was dressed in a full-length dress of palest lavender. Her black shoes barely showed at their toe tips. The dress had a lovely wide white collar with a small ruffle surrounding it. Around her shoulders was draped the loveliest crocheted triangular woolen shawl with fringe, and its color was of the same pale lavender as her gracefully slim dress.

Aunt Ella stood there, white silken hair piled high on top of her head, skin milk-white and draping softly like the folds of her dress, while around her aristocratic neck, which she held like a queen, was a one inch wide black velvet ribbon on which she had pinned a lovely cameo. Perhaps I remember her above all others in the room that evening because she looked so understatedly elegant, or perhaps because of her exclamation to my beaming mother. "<u>Millie</u>! You have rouge on that child's face! You must take it off!" I don't remember my mother's having followed the instructions, but I still feel Aunt Ella's reprimand!

That was considerably more than fifty years ago, this being 1984. There was lots of color for me in that moment; the lavender dress and shawl, and my pink dress and pink cheeks, and the flush on mother's face! Everything else about that room and that moment and that night seems grey.

The blue of March skies in my early days seems next most heightened in pure color. . . I used to sit on the window seat in our living room and look out at the clouds which passed overhead, dulling the spring sunlight momentarily, then passing on to the north with the winds. Somehow the warmth of that special sunlight seems full of color, and the contrasting blue of the sky seemed cold and sharp. The wheat fields in the distance took on that wonderful bright green of the season, and I love to remember watching those passing clouds, the sky and the wheat field across from Belford Church, which was as far away as I could see from my vantage point.

There seems so much color in life today! The TV programs are almost all in color, except when they're playing an oldie or excerpts from the first days of the medium. Colorful clothes fill the showrooms of large department stores and the windows of the lovely ladies' shops. Silkworms must be working overtime; there are so many choices of dresses, suits and blouses and scarves in any beautiful color and hue one can imagine, in designs both beautiful and startling! At the florists and nurseries today one can get hydrangeas and roses and rhododendron and peonies and dahlias and daisies in such stirring colors of such depth of tone one could believe that paint has been added to the blossoms. There are acrylics and oils and watercolors available to the artist for painting that Rembrandt would not have understood in his dark basement where he strained to mix his wonderfully rich dark colors.

Today, special companies have tank trucks for spraying fertilizer in the right quantities and richnesses to make lawns green, green, green. Automobiles come in as many colors as Easter eggs. Modern art knows no restraints in colors or abstractions. Decorators use their imaginations at full capacity to decorate rooms with fabrics which know no limitations in colors and coordinating accessories. Houses are filled with objects of art and plantings and atriums sporting the most beautiful of camellias and roses and brightly blooming flowers. Carpeting ranges from the most beautiful of oriental patterns to palest blues, pinks, yellows and deepest colored piles of bright red or any other color one could dream of. Kitchens sport conveniences like refrigerators and stoves and telephones that are no longer white enamel, but any color on earth. Kitchens can be equipped all in the same color or in every color of the spectrum at once! Life inside one's home today can be lived in color harmony or psychedelic disharmony like the insides of a kaleidoscope!

As I look back through the years, I see my earlier days in much less color than the ones I am now experiencing. If one wanted to, he might say, in reality that the "old days" were certainly more colorless for most people on this earth; today is brightened up to near capacity of exuberance. It is not just that I am more aware of color in the present; color is actually here today in inundating quantities! Contemporary photography has really heightened the color of its recordings, but I can look back to the days through which I have passed with less color and I see them in beautifully muted beauty. The browns and the greys and the dull greens and the pale pinks and lavenders and blue of other years seem at this point in retrospect more beautiful than ever!

I guess it is really like having lived in two different worlds. I think I'm truly fortunate to have realized this!

* * *

As I look back on the days we spent together as a family in our "house at the edge of the woods" on Rolling Fork, I have the loveliest feeling of warmth and color, and love weaves them into a soft, beautiful and comforting blanket. My wish is that my children, through reading these notes from their childhood and the life that we shared, find a kind of peace and security which permeates their lives. There is color in this beautiful family experience. It is the color of love and gives me much happiness today, as always.

Mother
October, 2004

* * *

Homemade Flower Arrangement